T0129028

Just
for
My
Journey

Just for My Journey

Expressions on My Walk

Diana B. Simpson

JUST FOR MY JOURNEY
EXPRESSIONS ON MY WALK

Copyright © 2018 Diana Simpson.

All rights reserved. No part of this book may be used or reproduced by any means, graphic, electronic, or mechanical, including photocopying, recording, taping or by any information storage retrieval system without the written permission of the author except in the case of brief quotations embodied in critical articles and reviews.

Scripture quotations marked KJV are from the Holy Bible, King James Version (Authorized Version). First published in 1611. Quoted from the KJV Classic Reference Bible, Copyright © 1983 by The Zondervan Corporation.

iUniverse books may be ordered through booksellers or by contacting:

iUniverse
1663 Liberty Drive
Bloomington, IN 47403
www.iuniverse.com
1-800-Authors (1-800-288-4677)

Because of the dynamic nature of the Internet, any web addresses or links contained in this book may have changed since publication and may no longer be valid. The views expressed in this work are solely those of the author and do not necessarily reflect the views of the publisher, and the publisher hereby disclaims any responsibility for them.

Any people depicted in stock imagery provided by Getty Images are models, and such images are being used for illustrative purposes only. Certain stock imagery © Getty Images.

ISBN: 978-1-5320-4758-9 (sc)
ISBN: 978-1-5320-4759-6 (e)

Library of Congress Control Number: 2018904535

Print information available on the last page.

iUniverse rev. date: 06/26/2018

Dedicated to

To my Father and Mother who established my existence
David and Mary

To my brothers and sisters, who love me with an unfaltering persistence
William, Cameron, Alexandre, Leslie, David, and Cynthia

To my spiritual leaders who gave me inspiration, so the words could flow freely
Bishop Mark and Mother Dorothy Walden

To the woman who gave me unconditional love, so completely
Precious Mother Dear

To my sisters who provided advice and inspiration very discretely
Leslie Davis and Shiela Keaise

To all who encouraged me and knew God could do it through me, I love you deeply

Contents

PRAISE AND WORSHIP

PRAYER

REPENTANCE

SALVATION

SANCTIFICATION

SERVITUDE

THANKFULNESS

TRUST

VICTORY

WISDOM

Preface

Tick, tock, I watched the clock. The seconds grew into minutes, the minutes to hours, the hours to days and the days to years. I remember the beginning of this journey. I can't say it felt like yesterday because it doesn't. It feels as though years have passed, and they have!

Many memories are stored in my psyche regarding my yearning to write. I can plainly recollect, as a child, my words were few. Often, I would sit in solitude and silence and reflect on a plethora of topics that were limited to my realm of carnal perspectives. As a result, they remained embedded in the four corners of my mind.

As my maturation evolved, I began to express my thoughts, feelings, and desires with pen and paper. As I reminisce, I can visualize sitting in my fifth-grade class passionately writing my essay on Dr. Martin Luther King Jr. I even recall my last words – "A Drum Major for Justice". Hence, there grew my thirst for transcribing. So, I wrote on matters that were pertinent to my existence as a person who struggled with being exposed to two worlds. In one realm, I would visit the Diamond Club to meet famous baseball stars such as Willie Mays, Ed Charles, and Roy Campanella at an Old Timers game at Shea Stadium. On the other hand, I would go to 40 Projects with my Mother to get goods that were given to low-income families. I can still taste the oily peanut butter in my mouth. My writings were fueled by my worldly experiences.

Little did I realize, a new fondness was beginning to formulate. My church-going neighbors, Ms. Reavis and Ms. Blake, provided me with my formal introduction to sanctification. It is now evident to me that indeed some plant. Then the watering began, in Walterboro, South Carolina, I witnessed the fruits of holy living from Aunt El and my Mother Dear. Then in Thomson, Georgia, I received my personal introduction to the Holy Ghost. As the Bishop laid his hands on me, my life was changed instantaneously, as was my penchant for writing. No longer did my writings reflect my earthly viewpoints but my yearning to attain heavenly goals and aspirations.

Consequently, my hands clicked on my computer keys, night and day, revealing what my spirit sought to say. My heart expressed what my spoken words failed to say. My writings foretold of the manner in which I am coming to know God. It has revealed a temporary encounter that was momentary but is proving to be everlasting. This is my revelation that God gives the increase.

So, I have come to understand that God's timing is not our timing. His timing is always the right time. I thought this book would have been completed over 15 years ago; but, I have come to realize that you have to wait on God!

Thus, these are just words on this Christian journey. In order for this compilation to have blossomed into its fullness, I had to endure the storm. So, here it is: Just for My Journey: Expressions on My Walk. They are words just for God, just for the people of God, and just for my journey.

Blessings

For thou, LORD, wilt bless the righteous; with favor wilt thou compass him as with a shield. Psalms 5:12

The Greatest Blessing

Some say I reflect too deeply, some say I think too much;
I'm not sure if I neglected my blessing or did I miss your touch?
I wonder if I missed my blessing or did it just go by;
Maybe if I reach again I can give it another try.
I'll look towards the sky, for I know it is very near;
But, first, I must have the Creator, for I know He cares.
See I can get a blessing quick, that isn't hard to attain;
But to get a dose of the Living God, from evil I must abstain.
So I'll ask you Dear Savior, for something I never had before;
Please Lord, help me walk close to you, even the more.
Let me humble myself, and totally give up my wicked ways;
I truly long to be sincere, in these last and evil days.
I want to praise you genuinely and be committed to your word;
Not just a hearer, but a doer, to all that I have heard.
Restore the joy of my salvation, tell me what to do;
Forgive me Lord, I'm sorry, for not totally trusting in you.
My focus was on man, and my vision was not very clear;
Being good so you'll love me, but that's not getting me there.
I want to feel you in my heart, I want you to be a friend to me;
I want it to run so deeply; I'll do anything just to please thee.
Someone said that blessings are the abundance of material things;
The greatest one for me is to have you as my one and only King.

And all these blessings shall come on thee, and overtake thee, if thou shalt hearken unto the voice of the Lord thy God. Deuteronomy 28:2

Setting Me Up!

Setting me up for a blessing, oh, the road that I had to take;
I lay awake with tears in my eyes, my heart wanted to break.
Thinking you did not love me, when folks began to walk away;
I questioned your omnipotence and didn't know what to say.
I heard your voice as a whisper, "Be still, I'll work it out";
I was too despondent and all I did was scream and pout.
You've always been my rescuer, as years go by, it's clearer to me;
But in the beginning, it's not something that I could visibly see.
Friends surrendered to a game that left tracks on their arms;
But you've been my protector, keeping me safe from all harm.
Many contracted AIDS, nestled in a soft sea of satin sheets;
You didn't let it happen, you said the odds I would beat.
Setting me up for a blessing, while others passed me by;
I would lay awake, late at night and all I could do was cry.
I began to doubt your sovereignty, as if I thought above you;
I never envisioned all the things, you were about to do.
I'm in awe over your mercy; it's so special and kind;
It's your unmerited favor, such a gift that blows my mind.
Taking time with all of your children, gentle Father you are;
Your ears always hear when I call, your arms stretch so far.
Satan kept trying to destroy me, setting his traps and snares;
You kept saying abide in me, be not dismayed and have no fear.
Satan seemed like he had me, didn't seem like I'd make it through;
You are an on-time God, once again you came to my rescue.
Setting me up for a blessing, my eyes were blinded by carnality;
I wasn't walking by faith, I wasn't even walking in victory.
Then, I began applying the word and did just what it said;
No longer bound in chains, not the tail, now I'm the head.

The blessing of the Lord, it maketh rich, and he addeth no sorrow with it. Proverbs 10:22

Commemorations

Praise ye the LORD. Praise God in his sanctuary: praise him in the firmament of his power. Psalms 150:1

What Christmas Means to Me

Been counting down this day, since last year;
Someone told me this is the season of good cheer.
Got up early this morning, so I can catch every sale;
Received so many circulars, in the morning mail.
I am on my way to visit, every single department store;
I'm not celebrating my birthday, so what is this all for?
Gathering around the Christmas tree, it looks so bright;
Stayed up late last night, trimmed it with such beautiful lights.
Presents stacked so high, hoping the day would hurry and come;
The more gifts I get, the more I will want to be given some.
We receive presents and get everything and more than asked for;
Deep inside, I know that the day must mean something more.
A big belly man, dressed in a suit, sparkling and shiny red;
Sliding down a chimney, Mama says we must be early to bed.
Cookies and milk set out, because during the night he will arrive;
This waiting game is torturing me; I don't think I can survive.
Santa represents a tradition, that's been around for a while;
I need to know more, somebody tell me about the Christ child.
Born in a manager so meek and mild, no crib to lay His head;
Born on Christmas day, hay and stubble is what cushioned His bed.
He was sent to live and die, so that eternal life could be mine;
Never even sinned, but by His precious blood He paid my fine.
God gave His only begotten Son, so that my spirit could be free;
Now I know what Christmas really means, my Savior is the key!

Now the birth of Jesus Christ was on this wise: When as his mother Mary was espoused to Joseph, before they came together, she was found with child of the Holy Ghost. Matthew 1:18

It's Christmas Time Again

By late October, decorations and lights have flooded the whole place;
Everyone is dazzled and amazed, the excitement shows on their face.
Children ride in cars, pointing to houses, shining bright with festive cheer;
Radios blast carols, we joyfully sing along to what we hear.
The stores are crowded with customers, looking for the best buys;
Shoppers tire easily waiting in line, exhaling a bunch of long sighs.
Bargain hunters snatching and grabbing, waking early before daylight;
Not showing an ounce of kindness, or attempting to do what's right.
Stop and ask yourself the reason for the season, I'm sure you will reply;
It's about a child who was born on Christmas day and here is the reason why.
He came to Earth to save us, from our sins and reconcile us to our Creator;
He took on the form of a man, no sacrifice could be found, for He is greater.
He lived and died so that we might have life, which is more than your shopping pleasure;
He wants you to store up heavenly riches, so you'll partake of His eternal treasures!

Yet it pleased the LORD to bruise him; he hath put him to grief: when thou shalt make his soul an offering for sin, he shall see his seed, he shall prolong his days, and the pleasure of the LORD shall prosper in his hand. Isaiah 53:10

The Best Is Yet to Come!

I've often heard it said that the best is yet to come;
I chose to ignore this, since I know where I'm from.
No illuminating lights, with my name enclosed within;
No dazzling diamonds, to adorn my beautiful skin.
Something deep inside, resonates loud and strong;
As I hear an inner voice saying "It won't be long."
Your latter will be greater, I knew you from the start;
I've put Me inside you, and from it you can't part.
I gave you the gift of life and with it you've done well;
As you continue on this journey, time will surely tell.
You've stood the test in the background, yet you did shine;
And now it's your season, the world will know you're mine.
The best is yet to come, I'm not a man that I should lie;
I'll pour you out a blessing, and it will only multiply.
Keep your eyes on me, I'll supply every one of your needs;
Your harvest is ripe and ready, for you have planted good seeds!

*And Joseph placed his father and his brethren, and gave them a possession in the land of Egypt,
in the best of the land, in the land of Rameses, as Pharaoh had commanded. Genesis 47:11*

Let Music Ring ....

When music rings, the peace of God prevails so still;
The Holy Spirit is welcomed, as we yield to His will.
The children of Israel sang, after the Lord parted the Red Sea;
Overjoyed with His glorious triumph, when He set them free.
To hear a word from the Lord, music helped the prophets plan;
A divine message was obtained, to heal the failing land.
An evil spirit departed from Saul, when Little David played;
Saul was refreshed and renewed, the enemy could not stay.
Music ushers The Spirit of God, in this Holy Place;
Demons are tormented and scurry, leaving without a trace.
The presence of Jehovah floods the temple completely;
Strumming Sounds of the guitar play on so sweetly.
A sin sick sinner's soul surrenders as he comes to the Lord;
Heaven rejoices, singing praises loudly, "Welcome Aboard."
When music rings, chains crumple, and the captive is released;
Heaven smiles upon us, for God is well pleased!

It came even to pass, as the trumpeters and singers were as one, to make one sound to be heard in praising and thanking the Lord; and when they lifted up their voice with the trumpets and cymbals and instruments of musick, and praised the Lord, saying, For he is good; for his mercy endureth for ever: that then the house was filled with a cloud, even the house of the Lord. 2 Chronicles 5:13

Just an Appreciation

This special day has been set aside, to show the musicians our sincere admiration;
Their labor of love hasn't gone unnoticed, so we merrily share in this joyous celebration.
Just an appreciation, an attempt to express how much we really care;
No words, deeds, or gifts can ever compensate, for all the things they bear.
They untiringly give their best, overflowing with an abundance of dedication;
They've inspired us all, heeding their call, expecting no monetary compensation.
With humble hearts, they play glorifying our awesome God beyond measure;
As we lend a listening ear, we sit in amazement of such a harmonious treasure.
The anointing floods the room, setting the atmosphere for blessings in this Holy place;
The strums of the strings launch us, in a whirlwind as the expressions show on our face.
The toot of the flute calms with soothing sounds, that relax every one of our reservations;
As the drums loudly resonate, our toes tap to its tune without any hesitations.
The organ blares with a foot stomping, soul saving pounce, that makes us let out a shout;
As the keyboard plays so mightily, summoning spirits that are being cast out.
The Shekinah Glory comes down, with a manifestation that is so strong;
The power of the anointing radiates, as you minister through your songs.
This is just an appreciation, for we care so much for you;
We can only offer you these tokens just to say, "Thanks for all you do!"

And he hath put a new song in my mouth, even praise unto our God: many shall see it, and fear, and shall trust in the LORD. Psalm 40:3

Never a Good-Bye

It's hard to say goodbye to an angel, who has constantly been by your side;
So, you simply cherish the memories, and lock them deep inside.
Yes, you will shed many tears, but the pain will eventually subside;
For she has served, for so many years, as a loving mentor and guide.
You know you will see each other again, so this is never a farewell;
From time to time you'll exchange short anecdotes, which you will tell.
Though things will be different, you'll reminisce on the past;
Laughing as you remember, all the fun you thought would last.
Sometimes a smile will cross our face, as we think of the joy we shared;
Friends are hard to find, when I recollect how much you cared.
Sometimes I may just start to cry, when I think of how I miss you so;
The hardest part of it all, was I didn't tell you I was scared of letting go.
So, I won't say good-bye; for to the future we are saying hello!

The LORD bless thee, and keep thee: The LORD make his face shine upon thee, and be gracious unto thee: The LORD lift up his countenance upon thee, and give thee peace. Numbers 6:24-26

What's Next?

Many ask what can come next, when a great task has been achieved;
Often overlooking all the blessings, which they have received.
This journey has taught me so very much, and this I can tell;
After all that I've been through, I can respond that it is well.
God has been so good to me and through it all, He has been there;
The load was never heavy, for He never put more on me than I can bear.
What's next? That was your question, well let me make this clear;
The Lord is my light and my salvation, of whom shall I fear?
He has thoughts of peace towards me, to give me an expected end;
Through it all, He has been my constant provider and my closest friend.
So, I don't fret about what's next, He has done so much for me;
No need to question tomorrow, for I know who holds the key.
What's next? There are only wonderful things, for on Him I do rely;
I've taken up my cross to follow Him, and my will I do deny!

And this is the will of Him that sent me, that every one which seeth the Son, and believeth on Him, may have everlasting life: and I will raise him up at the last day. John 6:40

Time of Positioning

You are not retiring, you are merely changing your position;
Not of your own doing, but it is the Lord's decision.
Working in the vineyard, as He has called you to do;
Giving of yourself, when so much is required of you.
Sometimes slowing your pace, in well-doing you must not tire;
Be reassured, it is God who has purified you in the fire.
As you begin to seek his face, your elevation will start;
As He orders your steps, you will have a change of heart.
The load will begin to get easy, for His burdens are light;
To the things you were once blind, you will now have sight.
Revelations will begin to manifest, like never before;
And you shall be blessed, with all the things God has in store!

And the LORD said unto Moses, Rise up early in the morning, and stand before Pharaoh; lo, he cometh forth to the water; and say unto him, Thus saith the LORD, Let my people go, that they may serve me. Exodus 8:20

A New Chapter

............ಌ·ಾ·ಾ❈⊙❈ಾ·ಾ·ಌ............

I'm starting a new chapter, I'm blessed to be moving ahead;
Many years have passed, this is the place that I have been led.
There are things I'm leaving behind, I no longer need them now;
I'll miss them for a little while, but the days will grow sweeter somehow.
I'll think of all the fond memories, as the pages stay etched on the lines;
They will sometimes bring a smile, as they flip throughout my mind.
I may even shed some tears, I never promised I wouldn't cry;
These were the best times of my life, so I'll just wave and say good-bye.
I've made an acquaintance or two, we'll stay close throughout the rest of the trials;
Though there have been some experiences, every single situation has been worthwhile.
I'm starting a new chapter, I'm so glad that it is finally here;
I'll passionately treasure this moment, for to me it is so dear.
Undertaking new endeavors, where wisdom will be my closest friend;
I'll embrace her wholeheartedly, until my days doth end.
I'm beginning this innovative chapter, it's so different from the rest;
For this time, I'm a bit wiser, and I'm assured to give my best!

............ಌ·ಾ·ಾ❈⊙❈ಾ·ಾ·ಌ............

Remember ye not the former things, neither consider the things of old. Isaiah 43:18

Welcome to Our Church

From the pastor to the little children, we're so glad you came;
Greetings to all, you are welcome to praise His Holy name.
Filled and running over, hold out your cup and you'll receive;
Those who come to Jesus, in Him you must only believe.
An open invitation, this is what the Savior has just for you;
No need for hesitation, for His love is pure and true.
He gave it to the Jews, but they rejected Him as God's Son;
He offered it to the Gentiles, sealed when He said it was done.
He's bidding all to come, from the highways near and far;
All you have to do is knock, for the door is always ajar.
He's waiting for you with His open arms, stretched wide;
Come running, safely to Christ, for in Him you can abide.
An open invitation, it is freely given, so freely receive;
The way you came, is definitely not, the way you'll leave.
The Redeemer, The King, today, He can truly set you free;
The Holy Ghost is in charge, here to bless you and me.
He has no respect of person, why not heed the call?
It is not just for some, but He has presented it to all.
The day you hear His voice, He said harden not your heart;
Nothing can separate you from His love, He will never depart.
So, enjoy the service, and be sure to put in, so you can get out;
The Lord is here to bless you, in Him you should have no doubt.
Welcome to our church, where we're winning souls to Christ;
This is the day the Lord has made, one that'll change your life.
So, it is not just by chance, that you've walked through these doors;
God has ordained your presence, for He has your miracle in store!

Praising God, and having favour with all the people. And the Lord added to the church daily such as should be saved. Acts 2:47

Welcome to the House of the Lord

Welcome to the House of the Lord,
Where the Spirit of the Lord does faithfully dwell;
You shall receive a word from the Lord,
For preached is the message of Holiness or Hell.
You've obeyed His voice and entered the gates,
This is where you're ordained to be;
We are gathered on one accord,
The Holy Spirit will deliver souls and set the captive free.
To save the world, not to condemn, closer than a brother,
He'll be your best friend;
You've heard this before, you've given up on love,
Your broken heart He wants to mend.
Welcome to the place of healing,
The way you've come is not the way you will leave;
Open up your heart, mind, and soul,
To the blessings of the Lord you can readily receive.
With loving kindness has He drawn thee,
The Spirit of the Lord is pulling you nigh;
This is more than just a welcome,
It's an opportunity to become a son of the Most High!

I am the door: by Me if any man enter in, he shall be saved, and shall go in and out, and find pasture. John 10:9

Resurrection Sunday

Pagan traditions, Satan's deceptions, a plan to make it all seem like a tale;
A misguided plot, suddenly stopped, since the gates of Hell cannot prevail.
Jesus proclaimed, the Word does not change, the grave was not meant for me;
On the third day I'll rise, all power is mine, to Hell I now hold the key.
Death defeated, the Devil felt cheated, he wouldn't have wanted Jesus crucified;
No relief, the pain didn't cease, on the will and the way of His Father He relied.
In the ninth hour, screamed and hollered, My God, why have I been forsaken by thee?
The sins of the world, I must bear them alone, so, all the world can be free.
My dear Son, it is done, by your blood all have been bought with a price;
Your life has sufficed, man reconciled to God by Christ, the ultimate sacrifice!

But God commendeth his love toward us, in that, while we were yet sinners, Christ died for us.
Romans 5:8

Deliverance

*The righteous cry, and the LORD heareth, and
delivereth them out of all their troubles.*
Psalms 34:17

The Need to Be Delivered

I need to be delivered, from the evil that lies within;
Familiar spirits keep calling me, from the places I've been.
Reminding me of the pleasures, in which I used to engage;
But I hear the Lord summoning me, to a place of higher praise.
I desire to heed the call, but my flesh is fighting to live;
To crucify the sinful cravings, is taking all, I can give.
I've fasted and prayed continuously, seems like it wants to stay;
So now I come to You Lord, asking You to make a way.
It's not Your will, for us to be bound in shackles and chains;
So, I lift my hands to thee, then these shackles can't remain.
All my life I wanted, an earnest and closer walk with thee;
So, I will listen very carefully, as I hear Your voice speak.
Examine yourself my child, forget all about the rest;
Is there anything too hard for God? This is only a test.
Stay with Me, and I AM will definitely set you free;
No heights, nor depth, can separate you from Me.
You need to be delivered, and I will do it, only ask;
Just stand, Jehovah-Mephalti, can accomplish any task!

And God sent me before you to preserve you a posterity in the earth, and to save your lives by a great deliverance. Genesis 45:7

Die Daily

Die daily, the word says this is what I must do;
Yet, this is the process, because it's making me new.
Stripping me to the core, wondering what else I will see;
I must pass this test, because I can't go back to where I used to be.
Die daily, then the Holy Spirit can have free reign;
With His constant guidance, from sin I will abstain.
Applying the scriptures, so that I'll be able to make it through;
Die daily, Lord my desire is to be just like you!

I am crucified with Christ: nevertheless I live; yet not I, but Christ liveth in me: and the life which I now live in the flesh I live by the faith of the Son of God, who loved me, and gave Himself for me. Galatians 2:20

Dip Me Again!

Oh, to be Holy Ghost dipped again, is all that I ask of thee;
Nothing is greater than the bond, shared between You and me.
I searched for the utmost approval, from every living man;
But now, I'm seeking direction, through your eternal divine plan.
I looked to please all others, but never was I thinking of You;
Now, I'm looking directly to You Jesus, to tell me what to do.
The Holy Ghost is a keeper, but I acted like I didn't know;
Constantly shunning His guidance, and steadily believing my foe.
Now I come to You Jesus, asking for this gift from above;
Please descend on me Comforter, like a mighty white dove.
Forgive me for not being steadfast, I moved at my every whim;
Never letting You guide me, now my pathway is very dim.
Dip me again, connected by the Spirit is how to live Your way;
Then, I'll totally trust and rely on You, each and every day!

I indeed have baptized you with water: but He shall baptize you with the Holy Ghost. Mark 1:8

No Longer Bound

I've tried so hard to do things, to please those in the world;
See my Dad always told me; you have to be a good little girl.
So, I gave to people and I seldom ever said no;
Now Lord, I come to You, because it's time for me to let go.
I want to run this race with patience, and be steadfast;
I must endure forever, for I want my freedom to last.
I am forgiving all offenses, so You can forgive me;
I am glad that You opened my eyes, now I can see.
I've been holding some things, they've been getting me down;
I'm releasing those things, I no longer want to be bound.
I want the Spirit to move freely, and have free course;
So, I'm emptying out my heart, and letting You be the source.

I am the Lord thy God, which have brought thee out of the land of Egypt, out of the house of bondage. Exodus 20:2

911 Emergency

I've never really needed anyone before;
Closed everyone out and shut the door.
Right now, my eyes are looking towards the sky;
The tears are building, and I want to cry.
Prior to this dilemma, I'm sorry I didn't call;
Somehow, I thought that I could handle it all.
Cast your cares on Me, is hard for me to believe;
Surely that's why Your aid, I could not receive.
Summoning everyone, and asking what do they think?
Never knowing, You were my one and only true link.
Now, I'm here with my heart overflowing with pain;
All I want to ask is, can You help with the strain?
Forgive me for not making You my number one;
I got caught up, and just wanted to have fun.
Here I am, because things just aren't straight;
I don't want to lose You, hope I'm not too late.
I'm calling to You, knowing that You'll answer me;
Please loose the chains, and set the captive free.
I know that You love me, so very much;
Right now, I'm in need, of Your soothing touch.
So here I come, on my bending knee;
I'll make this request, this is my plea, 911 Emergency!

(For He saith, I have heard thee in a time accepted, and in the day of salvation have I succoured thee: behold, now is the accepted time; behold, now is the day of salvation.) 2 Corinthians 6:2

Press to Jesus

I must press to Jesus, for in Him lies the evident cure;
So many witnesses can testify, of that I am sure.
Healing hands He possesses, I'll call them one by one;
Faith is the key, for it gets the job fully done.
The woman with the issue of blood, on no one to rely;
Touched His hem, when she saw Jesus passing by.
"Who touched me?" Christ cried, since many were about;
I felt the virtue depart, now your belief has brought you out.
Press to Jesus, for in Him I can find my true transformation;
I need only look to Him, to get the necessary consolation.
The centurion's servant lie sick with palsy, in a tormented state;
I am not worthy for You to come, but being healed is his fate.
You can restore him from here, Lord speak and he will be whole;
For You have great authority, I trust You with my heart and soul.
Press to Jesus, that is what I have heard others do and say;
Lord, You are the ultimate healer and I'm asking You on this day.
Lord have mercy on us, two blind men followed Him and declared;
We believe in Your miraculous power, of it we are assuredly aware.
Your belief is what has set you free, sightless eyes can now see;
These are some of the benefits, when you put your confidence in Me.
Press to Jesus, not a man that He should lie, no need to ever repent;
Think on His Word, more than able to do that for which He was sent.
You might say these happened long ago, it's not the same somehow;
He did it back then "Who are your eyewitnesses that can speak now?"
One day I was sinking deep in sin, bound to spend eternity in hell;
Jesus saw fit to spare my life, now in Heaven I'll forever dwell.
I am a walking miracle, let your eyes look me over and reflect;
God will do the same for you, for people He has no respect.
Press to Jesus, are you not confident in the things He can do?
Cry out and He will fulfill every promise that He has for you!

When she had heard of Jesus, came in the press behind, and touched His garment. For she said, if I may touch but His clothes, I shall be whole. Mark 5:27-28

Renew My Mind Jesus

Renew my mind Jesus, let me think on things that are pure;
Letting the old things pass away, then I will be able to endure.
Renew my mind Jesus, let me think of thoughts lovely and true;
For it is the Kingdom of Heaven, that I will forever seek to pursue.
Renew my mind Jesus, let me meditate on all that is real;
Then I'll be able to walk according to the Word, not by what I feel.
Renew my mind Jesus, I want to think about only the best;
When I am faced with adversities, I'll be able to pass any test.
Renew my mind Jesus, let me think on things as You would do;
Caring for my neighbor, I see daily, as I profess I worship You.
Renew my mind Jesus, let every thought come from agape love;
Then the Holy Spirit, can descend on me like a mighty dove.
Renew my mind Jesus, then I can do the things You want me to;
Otherwise, I'm like a tinkling cymbal, and my fate is doomed.
Renew my mind Jesus, my ultimate desire is to serve You every day;
Please renew my mind, for it is how I can earnestly fast and pray!

And be not conformed to this world: but be ye transformed by the renewing of your mind, that ye may prove what is that good, and acceptable, and perfect, will of God. Romans 12:2

The God I Serve...

The God I serve is so awesome, I wonder if you know;
When the storms are raging, it's to Him I humbly go.
He will calm the roaring seas, the winds and waves obey;
Peace be still, is all that the Master will have to say.
The God I serve is a healer, ask so many they will tell;
He says thy sins have been forgiven, and now all is well.
With just one touch of His garment or He can speak a word;
The lame walks, the blind sees, when His voice is heard.
The God I serve is a deliverer, I have seen what He can do;
Entangled in bondage, the Deliverer will bring you through.
From the hand of the enemy, you will be totally set free;
No respect of person, He'll do it for you, He'll do it for me.
The God I serve is a wonder, read the Bible, remove all doubt;
Then you'll know the God I serve, will always bring you out!

Only fear the LORD, and serve Him in truth with all your heart: for consider how great things He hath done for you. 1 Samuel 12:24

A Man Named Jesus

I knew you, even before your day of birth;
Called you into being, before I formed the Earth.
I watched you grow, since the days of your youth;
Put you on this road, to lead you to the truth.
Satan sought to kill and destroy you, I said not so;
My hand is upon your life, in time you will know.
Though the trials were many, I never let you down;
Every time you called, I always came around.
Through the heartache and pain, I dried your tears;
As you lifted your eyes to Heaven, I was right there.
Though you caused me pain, still I stood right by;
My love for you is everlasting, on me you can rely.
Perish in your sins, that is not my wish for any man;
Alpha and Omega, when it is impossible, I can!
You have tried everything else, give my love a try;
Unconditional and faithful, without it you will die.
I know you have been searching, this path leads to me;
I am the man named Jesus, I can set you free!

Jesus saith unto him, I am the way, the truth, and the life: no man cometh unto the Father, but by Me. John 14:6

Blinded Eyes See

He healed the sick and raised the dead;
With fish and loaves, five thousand fed.
But there is nothing more exciting to me;
Than the day He gave vision, when I couldn't see.
Jesus spat on clay and put it on a man's eyes;
The man was healed, to his neighbor's surprise.
He laid hands on a man, who saw men as trees;
"Go in peace and tell no one that I healed thee".
Blind men cried and pleaded, "Have mercy on me";
Christ simply replied, "If only ye can believe."
Spiritual sight causes me the most glee;
The songwriter said it best, blind but now I see.
If the blind lead the blind, they both shall fall;
One can't show the other, it isn't their call.
Clean your inner man first, so others know the way;
Ask God to purify you, to Him you must pray.
Psalms 51, can help you truly see the light;
For when God opens blinded eyes, there is true sight!

Then was brought unto Him one possessed with a devil, blind, and dumb: and He healed him, insomuch that the blind and dumb both spake and saw. Matthew 12:22

Eyes Have Not Seen

Eyes have not seen all that God has prepared for me;
Ears have not heard the things that will come to be.
His ways are so high, above the manner in which I behave;
His thoughts are so different, than those in which I engage.
There is none like Him, in Heaven or in Earth below;
When I am discouraged, it is to Him that I can go.
He has promised, He will be my constant friend;
He has assured me, it is upon Him I can depend.
I never imagined, I would find a Father so dear;
Even when I am unfaithful, He has been right there.
My heart has never felt a love, that is so pure and true;
His touch is so soothing, He knows just what to do.
I'm covered by His precious blood, in Him my protection lies;
In Him I've placed my trust, for He is sovereign and wise.
Eyes have not seen, what I shall earn if I remain with thee;
Nor ears have heard, what He has in store just for me!

But as it is written, Eye hath not seen, nor ear heard, neither have entered into the heart of man, the things which God hath prepared for them that love Him. 1 Corinthians 2:9

Just for You

I started to pray for you, but I got in the way;
So I began to say, I'll wait and try it another day.
You fell by the wayside, yet I'm still not interceding now;
I let you down, without God I can really see how.
So, caught up on power, ego tripping beyond belief;
Just avoided your needs, didn't know you needed relief.
Now I stand in shame, and I don't know what to do;
So, I'm asking God, to make both of us brand new.
I hate to see you in pain, somehow, I feel to blame;
I should have called Jesus, but I called every other name.
So, here I am, and I really just want to cry;
But that won't help, so I'll give it another try.
I'll ask Jesus to forgive me, for being so self-consumed;
I didn't realize without prayer, my life could be doomed.
So, I'll rely totally on God, only He has the power to release;
I'll just plant and water, because God gives the increase!

God hath spoken once; twice have I heard this; that power belongeth unto God. Psalm 62:11

Just Thinking

I wonder if God is mad with me;
Doors closed shut, my eyes can't see.
Lost in confusion, bound by fear;
Want to scream, God, are you here?
I am drowning in water, that's so deep;
Feels like I'm dying, so I just weep.
God have mercy, here I stand;
Precious Lord, please take my hand!
Be still my child, don't you fret;
Don't you know, I'm not through yet!
These light afflictions, won't last long;
When you are weak, then I am strong.
Don't you know, on me you can lean;
Have no fear, I'm on the scene.
According to My will, I'll perform the task;
I AM, will do, above all you can think or ask!

For who hath known the mind of the Lord? or who hath been His counsellor? Romans 11:34

In Solitude

In solitude, I waited, for an answer from you;
Please give me the solution, I'll do what I must do.
It's hard to wait patiently, I'd murmur and complain;
I felt like I was losing my mind, I thought I was going insane.
I felt so alone, and wondered if I could stand;
I longed for any advice, so I began to look to man.
No one had an answer, no one had the cure;
My faith began to waver, I felt so insecure.
Like a ship, I was tossed, on the raging sea;
All I could cry was Jesus, please come see about me.
Experiencing rebellion, totally beyond my belief;
Worse than witchcraft, I could not find any relief.
I began to get stubborn, longing for things to go my way;
Becoming disobedient, not listening to what God had to say.
In my solitude, I needed to find a way out;
First, I had to repent, to remove all fear and doubt.
I lifted my hands and cried Father, forgive me please;
Lord, I'm sorry; for it's my flesh, I've sought to appease.
He looked on me with mercy, as only a Father could;
He began to heal my insides, like I knew He would.
In my solitude, I found out, just how much He really cares;
I soon realized, that He was by my side, forever He'd be there.
Father, please allow this heart of repentance to remain;
My soul's salvation is most important, it's what I must maintain!

So the Lord alone did lead him, and there was no strange god with him. Deuteronomy 32:12

The Place I'm In

Never been in a place, like this before;
Seems so lonely, all closed doors.
This is new, so I don't know what to do;
So, I'll just stand firm and trust in You.
This place I'm in is so very strange;
Out of my comfort zone, out of my range.
I'm on this road, but I'm never alone;
You said that You are the Chief Cornerstone.
This place I'm in is really hard;
Suffering much, getting bruised and scarred.
Pain so deep, that I can't really comprehend;
Someone said broken hearts, You can mend.
I'll rely on You, while I'm in this place;
For every tear I shed, You said You'd erase!

For the Lord will not forsake His people for His great name's sake: because it hath pleased the Lord to make you His people. 1 Samuel 12:22

Life's Issues

Life's issues are overwhelming, is what we often say;
But the burdens become light, when we do it God's way.
There must be balance, God must be the head;
The Anointing will flow down from Him; if we can be led.
He is a God of decency and order; we must do our part;
Hidden iniquities, must be removed, that are clogging our heart.
We must repent, being Godly sorry, for all of our wrong;
Then, we can overcome, for in Him we can be strong.
Come boldly, to the throne of grace, for mercy in time of need;
We have a High Priest, touched by our infirmities, He will intercede.
Nevertheless, Thy will be done, must be our earnest request;
Petitions will be granted, for He hears what we confess.
Trials and tribulations will come, for they are a part of this Christian race;
All we have to do is humble ourselves and pray, seeking the master's face.
Then He will hear our cry, forgive us, and heal the land;
Then, we can walk circumspectly, understanding His divine plan.

Keep thy heart with all diligence; for out of it are the issues of life. Proverbs 4:23

Standing on My Own

I never thought it would come to this, and I never wanted it to;
I've tried my best, to do everything that I've known to do.
Now the road is getting rough, the climb is totally uphill;
The storm is raging so fierce, I'm crying, peace be still.
My enemies are laughing and saying where is God now?
But in this midst of confusion, I know You'll show up somehow.
They're saying aha, aha and declaring I'm losing my mind;
I just have to hold on to Your promises, You've proven to be so kind.
They say that I'm nothing and that I won't amount to be very much;
But I just can't forget the day You anointed me with Your special touch.
Yes, right now I'm standing alone, and the pain is very deep;
Tears are flooding my eyes, I continuously want to weep.
Joy comes in the morning, on the word of God I must rely;
He is the ultimate source, all my needs He will supply.
He is my Jehovah Jireh, I won't go lacking for anything;
He is my Elohim, He is the Creator of everything.
There is no one like Him, with Him I can stand on my own;
For He has assured me that He'll never leave me alone!

Hearken unto this, O Job: stand still, and consider the wondrous works of God. Job 37:14

Faithfulness

Jesus Christ the same yesterday, and today, and forever. Hebrews 13:8

The Promise of Faithfulness

Father God in Heaven, You are concerned about my every plea;
You are not so far, that You cannot come and see about me.
You love me so much, You gave Your only begotten Son;
As He hung on the cross, His final words were "It is done."
Now, everything I need, lies completely in these three words;
For now, I can speak with authority, all the promises I have heard.
There is nothing too hard for God, all I have to do is believe;
Every blessing He has for me, I can readily receive.
While I am speaking, You hear, and before I call, You reply;
If I ask, according to Your will, my earnest cry, you won't deny.
You are my closest friend, that sticks closer than a brother;
You care for me, when I am forsaken, by my father and mother.
You will never place a burden upon me, more than I can bear;
I can bring any problem to You, and leave it right there.
You will comfort me, when the load seems too much to carry;
Even when I fall, to the backslider, You are married.
What manner of love, that on Earth, man is above all things;
When a sinner comes to the Lord, the angels do sing.
I'm in awe over Your promises, so, I'm making one to You;
For the rest of my life, I'll live my life, the way You want me to!

Let us hold fast the profession of our faith without wavering; for He is faithful that promised.
Hebrews 10:23

On the Word

I've always wanted a house on a hill;
And enough money to pay the bills.
I've prayed for things, that money could buy;
Always failing, to give God a try.
I've looked to people, to be my guide;
Never knowing on Christ, I could rely.
My pain was deeper, than I care to share;
Of God's grace, I remained unaware.
So many promises, made to me by man;
Heartaches and agony, I could no longer stand.
I've always tried, to do things on my own;
Yet never liked the thought, of being alone.
Many things, I would do in the name of the Lord;
Little did I know, God was not on board.
Steadily attempting, to do all that I could;
Trying to win approval, just for being good.
My spirit was willing, but my flesh was weak;
I must talk to Jesus and listen when He speaks.
He told me, that I must surrender my all;
I may stumble, but He'd never let me fall.

It's up to me, to make my flesh behave;
Or it'll control me, I'll be its slave.
On Jesus, I must totally trust and depend;
Closer than a brother, He is my friend.
Praise and pray daily, is what I must do;
Worship HIM in spirit, is what makes it true.
God said "Love thy neighbor as thyself";
He wishes above all else, I'll prosper and be in good health.
Cattle on a thousand hills, He has infinite wealth;
Looking to the hills, from which cometh my help.
He said He'd keep me, because I cannot keep myself;
I will bless the Lord, and His praises, shall be in my mouth.
On Him I can rely, there is never any need to doubt;
He is my arch of safety, not a man that He should lie.
Putting my trust in Him, for on His Word, I can rely;
God will never leave me, nor forsake me, I'm not alone.
He that dwelleth, in the secret place, finds the strongest abode;
He's a very present help, in a time of need.
I'll look to Him, for the birds, He doth feed;
On the Word of God, I must stay.
For He shall always, direct my very way!

But He answered and said, It is written, Man shall not live by bread alone, but by every word that proceedeth out of the mouth of God. Matthew 4:4

Fight the Good Fight of Faith!

God told us, if we have faith, the size of a mustard seed;
We could do the impossible, if we can only believe.
Tell the mountain to move, it must get out of the way;
If we fall on our knees, humble ourselves, and pray.
Faith is the substance of things hoped for, the evidence of things we don't see;
Delve into the Spirit realm, for there are all the things, which will be.
Faith cometh by hearing, that which is God's word;
Open up your ears, so that His voice may be heard.
You must have faith to please Him, for He told us so;
Every promise you can receive, this is something you should know!

Fight the good fight of faith, lay hold on eternal life, whereunto thou art also called, and hast professed a good profession before many witnesses. 1 Timothy 6:12

Family

For the promise is unto you, and to your children, and to all that are afar off, even as many as the Lord our God shall call. Acts 2:39

Family So Dear

Family is so dear to me; I cannot tell it all;
Through the thick and thin, every time I call.
Our ties only strengthen, as the years go by;
We grow closer daily, here's the reason why.
The older ones share stories, of how it used to be;
We may begin to weep, or it fills our hearts with glee.
They tell us many things, that help us along our way;
We cherish their knowledge, and the wisdom they display.
The younger ones are our strength, their ideas are new;
They look upon life, as if there isn't anything, they can't do.
Trained up in the way they should go, from it, they won't depart;
We speak blessings upon their lives, they deserve the best start.
Now is the time we celebrate family, from far and near;
These are the days, God has ordained, this is crystal clear.
Let's laugh, and have merry moments, as we feast on cuisine and love;
The heavens are smiling, God is showering wonders from above.
Family, so dear to God, that He gave us His only begotten Son;
He saved us from our sins, His final words, "It is done."

And I will establish my covenant between Me and thee and thy seed after thee in their generations for an everlasting covenant, to be a God unto thee, and to thy seed after thee. Genesis 17:7

Father's Love

A father's love is gentle, a father's love is pure;
A father's love is patient, a father's love is sure.
It knows no boundaries, knows no concept of time;
It is forevermore, and upon it, you can always rely.
Love gave its only Son, for a lost sinner like me;
Releasing the bounds of sin, now indeed, I am free.
It went to Calvary's rugged cross, hung, bled, and died;
It took on the sins of the world, even was crucified.
The love did not end there, on the third day, it rose;
It even cradled me in its arms, when its love, I did oppose.
A Father's love is precious, I had my taste on Earth;
The man who loved me dearly, was there since my birth.
The story doesn't end, for he was my taste, of Heaven divine;
For he taught me the love of Jesus, is eternally mine!

Jesus answered and said unto him, If a man love Me, he will keep My words: and my Father will love him, and We will come unto him, and make Our abode with him. John 14:23

My Dad

He's always been a powerful pillar, on which I can depend;
Through the years, we've come to be the very best of friends.
More than a father to me, he's my closest ally;
Through the years, he has proven, on him I can rely.
The greatest teacher, I've ever had, he's taught me, so much;
During my trials, he eased my fears, with just the slightest touch.
Though sometimes, I let him down, he learned not to say a word;
Earnestly lifting, his voice to Heaven, his prayers they were heard.
Throughout my life, closely remaining, right here by my side;
Learning to encourage me, the truth he'd never hide.
Though my Dad, is up in years, and his pace has become measured;
His wisdom cannot be bought, it's my heavenly treasure.
His speech has become unhurried, yet his expressions, still remain strong;
He's given me admirable guidance, he's never led me wrong.
I love our conversations, whenever we can speak;
He listens so intensely, and his advice I'll continue to seek.
I love my Dad, so very much, and applaud his success;
I'd like for him to know, to me he is the best.
He thinks because his words are few, that they mean less to me;
He never shall imagine, just how they've set me free.
Dad, knows just what to do, to ease my troubled mind;
I hope Dad will always know, that he is one of a kind!

Hear, ye children, the instruction of a father, and attend to know understanding. Proverbs 4:1

A Praying Mama

Some people implore for riches, and wealth untold;
Others request, something tangible, that they can hold.
Several seek, to attain possessions, of rubies and gold;
Or pursue a fountain of youth, so, they'll never grow old.
Those are things, that I wanted, to desperately attain;
But those things are temporal, and they, just won't remain.
I need a heart to heart connection, with my loving Savior;
That's something, to definitely confirm my behavior.
God knew money, could never unconditionally suffice;
So, He gave me something costly, for which, there is no price.
He sent a Praying Mama, who goes on her bending knee,
And cries out to Heaven, and the Lord hears every plea.
The prayers of the righteous, truly avails much;
Constantly interceding for others, Heaven she does touch.
A Praying Mama, who awakes before the morning sun;
Petitioning the Lord, to let His perfect will be done.
A Praying Mama, can't compare, with this world's treasure;
For she is a jewel, for which none could ever measure!

And she said, Oh my lord, as thy soul liveth, my lord, I am the woman that stood by thee here, praying unto the Lord. 1 Samuel 1:26

You Are My Special Mom!

You tell me, I'm your special baby, and I believe that it's true;
But I think it's about time I say, just what I feel about you.
You are my special mom, God shows you just what I need;
Never too busy, that you won't bend your knees and intercede.
Ever since I've been saved, deliverance has been my humble appeal;
I saw you in my dreams, speaking the Word that did heal.
You embrace me with a gentle hug, when all is in disarray;
You know just what to say, to brighten my melancholy day.
I've been blessed with a spiritual mom, who knows how to get the job done;
You've imparted so much in me, in the spirit, I know I've already won.
You chastise and reprimand, when I'm getting out of my lane;
Doing it with compassion, thus, our relationship isn't strained.
I'm learning to live holy, and I thank God for your guide;
You only stand for holiness, never choosing any man's side.
I respect you wholeheartedly, for all the wonderful things you do;
God put me in your path, so, I can be a virtuous woman too.
Your heart has been cleansed, as you pray for all to make it through;
Words of wisdom you convey, for the fear of the Lord is inside you.
You preach the gospel with such power, all must come up to the mark;
The Holy Ghost controls as He erupts within you from a single spark.
You are my special mom, my true example of holiness on Earth;
Ministering to the saints always allowing us to see our genuine worth!

Honour thy father and mother; which is the first commandment with promise. Ephesians 6:2

Mothers

The Bible says: The effectual fervent prayers, of the righteous, avails much;
God has provided me with mothers, whose prayers Heaven doth touch.
Spiritual mothers, who boldly come, to the throne of grace;
Making their requests known, as they seek The Master's face.
Symbolizing the blessed Trinity - Holy Ghost, Father, and Son;
Constantly giving me guidance, I believe that the battle is won.
Located in three places, providing wisdom to set the captive free;
A little piece of Heaven on Earth, just to take care of me.
Words of wisdom, they speak, even before I utter a sound;
They clarify the situation, making it plain, as they clearly expound.
Spiritual mothers, who have come into my life, to impart holy proficiency;
Directing me, on this road to integrity, seeking to eliminate my deficiencies.
Yes, God has entrusted me, in your hand, for He knew, you would lead me right;
Thank you for being my spiritual mothers, being on call, whether it is day or night!

The elder women as mothers; the younger as sisters, with all purity. 1 Timothy 5:2

When My Mother and Father ...

When my Mother and Father forsake me, then, You said You'd take me in;
In You, I've found a resting place, against all odds, I can truly win.
You are my one true comfort, there is no other, that holds such a precious name;
With You I find contentment, none can accomplish the same!
When my friends are few, and I seem to be burdened down;
In You I have a hiding place, You promised, that You'd always be around.
Closer than a brother, You gave Your life, just to take my place;
In You, I find the strength and courage I need, to run this Christian race.
When my faith begins to fail, and it seems as if I can't stand on my own;
I AM has made this solemn vow, He'll never leave me alone.
Right now, my heart is breaking, and it seems as if all is totally lost;
Great God that You are, please keep equipping me, You are my unfailing source!

When my father and my mother forsake me, then the Lord will take me up. Psalm 27:10

Forever in Our Hearts

Forever in our hearts, you will always remain;
Our family chief, you will indefinitely reign.
The love we feel, one can never describe;
For you are a part, of our inner minds.
Seems like eternity, we've had you near;
For so long, you've eased our deepest fears.
How does one say farewell, to our patriarch?
Guiding us so long, through the cold and dark.
How does one express, what words cannot relate?
How does one describe, what we can't utter or say?
So simply stated, so plainly, and clearly proclaimed;
Your spirit will remain, your legacy will forever reign.
We can't say good-bye, so for now, we'll say farewell;
For God has assured us, that we will meet again!

Men and brethren, let me freely speak unto you of the patriarch David, that he is both dead and buried, and his sepulchre is with us unto this day. Acts 2:29

My Auntie

I'm sure being born in a family, has its many returns;
But adoption is so special, because it's a gift you can't earn.
God gave this special gift of acceptance to a Gentile like me;
It causes me to willingly smile and be filled with such glee.
You've taken me in as your own, words can't express how I feel;
For you have offered me true love, this is something that's real.
Some have sought to acquire gain, by saying they are sincere;
Actions speak much louder than words, for you've been right here.
You don't ridicule or cause me shame, you pray me right on through;
I'm so glad God put me in your path, He knew exactly what to do.
You have given so many things to me, that money can never buy;
Interceding for others, beckoning them to hear the Lord's cry.
There is nothing you have given, that the Lord will not restore;
You're building up your riches and treasures, in Heaven's store.
I admire your steadfastness, while standing in the gap for all;
I praise and thank God, that you willingly answered His call.
You are my Auntie, you're filled with such poise and grace;
So humble and obedient, you inspire me to seek God's face.
I respect the way you serve the Lord, secure in your place;
You are my sweet Auntie, the Lord exalts those who are abased!

Of whom the whole family in Heaven and Earth is named. Ephesians 3:15

Lean on Me Sisters

I'm your lean on me sister, I need for you to understand;
Whenever you call on me, I'll lend a helping hand.
I will stand by your side, whenever you're going through;
I make this earnest vow, I will continually be there for you.
I will help you accomplish goals, that you seek to achieve;
When I get a blessing, you know you can readily receive.
Situations have you down, and you're feeling sad;
Please don't get upset, there is no need to be mad.
One chases a thousand, ten thousand flee from two;
When we are in agreement, there's so much we can do.
Just call on me and I will give you some relief;
I can offer comfort through all of your grief.
Are you my lean on me sister? I believe that you are!
No matter if you are close, no matter if you're far.
I feel you will support me, through the thick and thin;
You'll give that extra push, when I seem to give in.
Like Mary and Elizabeth, we will be close as kin;
I can assist you in this Christian race, I trust that you'll win.
Lean on me sisters, that's what you and I will always be;
Have no doubts our bond is solid, that's a sure guarantee!

For where two or three are gathered together in My Name, there Am I in the midst of them.
Matthew 18:20

I Am A Child

I am a child of the King, so, I must stand tall;
He is able to keep me, He'll never let me fall.
In Him I find comfort, and my resting place;
I'm living this life, to one day see His face.
He won't forsake me, He's a friend indeed;
He is my Jehovah Jireh, supplying my every need.
I am a child of God, He calls me His very own;
He responds to my pleas, He consoles my every groan.
He loved me first, so now, I love Him too;
Please help me to do what is needed to follow you!
Help me to be a tree planted by the river, so I'll grow;
Allow my roots to go deeper, so I can feel the water flow.
I need a firm foundation, keep me grounded in your word;
Please open my spiritual ears, so, your voice can be heard.
I am a child of God, I'm the branch and He's the vine;
Help me to profess daily, oh how Jesus is mine!
I am a child of God, I'll let my little light shine;
The table is spread and with Him, I shall eternally dine!

The Spirit Itself beareth witness with our spirit, that we are the children of God. Romans 8:16

A Part of My Heart

I'm leaving a part of my heart, with it you'll know what to do;
Whenever I need to be close, I'll be right there with you.
Not asking you to watch, that request doesn't have to be made;
You've always prayed and interceded for me, now I'm out to give you aid.
You said I had the gift of help, didn't always believe what you said;
Repeatedly speaking to me, so within me, life you did embed.
Patiently you waited for me, while I received the Rhema word;
At first I just listened, now God's voice I have truly heard.
So, I'm leaving a part of my heart, nurture it so it will grow;
For in the years that follow, you'll reap whatever you sow.
You are my Naomi, you've taught me almost all that you had to give;
Now righteousness is deeply rooted and that's how I want to live.
A virtuous woman, you've been called to be that since birth;
My beloved Mama given to me, my treasure right here on Earth.
I love you so very dearly, for you adopted me as your own;
With love you drew me, knowing I didn't want to be left alone.
I'm leaving a part of my heart, that's the way I'll remain near;
You are my precious jewel, for you are my sweet Mother Dear!

And Ruth said, Intreat me not to leave thee, or to return from following after thee: for whither thou goest, I will go; and where thou lodgest, I will lodge: thy people shall be my people, and thy God my God. Ruth 1:16

Forgiveness

But I say unto you which hear, Love your enemies,
do good to them which hate you.
Luke 6:27

Forgiveness

Father forgive them, for they know not what they do;
Yet the ridicule didn't stop, as they continued to mock you.
Bearing the sins of mankind, none of them were Your own;
On a rugged cross, You died, agape love was shown.
Now, my brother offended me, and I am harboring disdain;
Knowing You can't forgive me, and Your Spirit won't remain.
So, help me to forgive, even before the offense takes place;
Father, against You I have sinned, now my transgression, please erase!

Then said Jesus, Father, forgive them; for they know not what they do. And they parted His raiment and cast lots. Luke 23:34

Forgive Me!

Lord forgive me, for all that I have done wrong;
Depending on myself, thought I was the one strong.
I seldom consulted You, about anything;
Oh, what sorrow, it did often bring.
Disobedience is worse than witchcraft to You;
I'm reaping the harvest, for what I did, and didn't do.
Forgive me, for walking in my evil ways;
Desiring the things of my flesh, now I have to pay.
You are a God of forgiveness, so, I make this earnest plea;
Against You I have sinned, so, I'm saying sorry to thee.
I admit that I have done wrong, I have no one else to blame;
Lord, I appreciate the way, You have spoken to my shame.
I have no excuse, for I knew The Word and what is right;
I chose to walk in darkness, and disregard the light.
I'm asking your forgiveness, please keep me in Your care;
Two masters I can't serve, my love I cannot share.
So, Lord, please forgive me, with You is where I want to be;
I love You so much, because You first loved me!

For if ye forgive men their trespasses, your Heavenly Father will also forgive you: But if ye forgive not men their trespasses, neither will your Father forgive your trespasses. Matthew 6:14-15

Tears I Cry

The tears I cry, run deep down inside;
And every day, they simply multiply.
No smile can ever hide, the way I feel;
This pain in my heart, seems too real.
I've tried to pretend, it doesn't exist;
Yet the aching, continues to persist.
Light afflictions, only last for a while;
Now, I'm wondering, am I still God's child?
Weeping lasts for a night, joy will come.
I don't know what to do, except runaway;
It solved things before, if only for a day.
I'm tired Lord, and I sincerely need aid;
According to my deeds, I'm getting paid.
It won't always be like this, so I'll wait;
For You are an on-time God, and never late!

Look upon mine affliction and my pain; and forgive all my sins. Psalm 25:18

Friendship

Wherefore comfort yourselves together, and
edify one another, even as also ye do.
1 Thessalonians 5:11

In Our Hearts

You have a style all your own, that no one could ever replace;
Such joy floods our souls, as you greet us, with your smiling face.
As you make your daily rounds, you radiate, as you stop to greet all;
This is one of your gifts from God, this definitely is your call.
Your compliments are my favorite, about what I'm wearing or my hair;
In my heart, I'm deeply touched, for you are the one, who possesses such flair.
How I admire your humble beginnings, you are my mentor and my guide;
Always giving God the glory, for you know it is Him, which has been on your side.
Giving a listening ear, even though so much, is required of you;
Never taking it for granted, that it was the Lord that carries you through.
Now and then, you were candidly honest, it hurt me deeply once or twice;
Faithful are the wounds of a friend, so the words forgive me, always did suffice.
Celebrating your many years of service, believing it was nothing but God's grace;
You will be missed, in more ways than you'll ever know, as you leave this place.
But the memories, remain deeply embedded, for in my heart, you have a special space!

Since thou wast precious in my sight, thou hast been honourable, and I have loved thee: therefore will I give men for thee, and people for thy life. Isaiah 43:4

Message for My Friend

We watched each other, make many mistakes;
Through the years, we suffered overwhelming heartaches.
So much faith, you had before life's tragedies;
You moved God's heart, you held the key.
Then one day, I heard a voice;
To heed the call, was my choice.
Living holy, is my reasonable sacrifice;
Now the Holy Spirit leads, I take His advice.
Now, I have but one gift for you;
Here is something, I can do.
Lead you to a savior, that answers a cry;
Your knock, He shall never deny.
So why don't you let Jesus, set you free;
You know better than anyone, what He did for me!

He that walketh with wise men shall be wise: but a companion of fools shall be destroyed
Proverbs 13:20

A Friend to Me!

Truly, you have been a friend to me;
And this is something that I have come to see.
Through the years, you have stood by my side;
Teaching me the Holy Spirit, is our one true Guide.
You mean more to me, than words could express;
Our friendship has withstood, the ultimate test.
Praying and interceding, when times were hard;
A true soldier, sometimes gets bruised and scarred.
Standing in the gap, the Spirit cleans hearts;
Walking the walk, living Holy is our part.
Purchased by the blood and cleansed, no more stains;
Sisters in Christ, we will always and forever remain.
Truly, you have showed yourself to be friendly;
So glad you intervened for me, on your bending knee.
I will always thank God, for sending you my way;
May God, forever bless you and yours, all your days!

A man that hath friends must shew himself friendly: and there is a friend that sticketh closer than a brother. Proverbs 18:24

From Then Until Now

From then until now, we've come this far;
God joined us together, knowing who we are.
He knew just what He had in mind;
Each one of us had something, He could find.
He gave one compassion and a heart of gold;
Another authority, to strengthen the hold.
One concern for all to make us real strong;
Another that the others would steer from wrong.
He knew we would need help to make it through;
God covered the friendship with love, to make it true!

Iron sharpeneth iron; so a man sharpeneth the countenance of his friend. Proverbs 27:17

What Is A Friend?

What is a friend? If indeed I may ask;
Someone to trust, when removing your mask.
Pain is felt through tears, that we can't hide;
Hoping it will ease our hurt, down deep inside.
What is a friend? I shall profoundly say;
Smiling faces, reassuring words, to make my day.
Watching and praying, as you become all you can;
God sent someone on whom you can depend.
A friend is family, a confidante, all wrapped in one;
A helper through the tests, until they are done.
A person on whom you can totally rely;
A trustworthy bond that you can't deny.
What is a friend? I found one faithful and true;
Friends for a lifetime, it will always be me and you!

Faithful are the wounds of a friend; but the kisses of an enemy are deceitful. Proverbs 27:6

Godliness

For bodily exercise profiteth little: but godliness is profitable unto all things, having promise of the life that now is, and of that which is to come. 1 Timothy 4:8

The Lord Is...

The Lord is my Shepherd, as well as my Guide;
His word in my heart, He told me to hide.
He is my constant Strength, He is my solid Rock;
He declared the door would open, if only I knock.
My Mediator, Provider, only begotten Son;
With You in my life, the battle is already won.
Alpha, Omega, the Beginning, the End;
Closer than a brother, my best Friend.
Lily of the Valley, Bright Morning Star,
More than words can express, that's what You are!
Well of Water, one drink – my thirst went away;
If I abide in You, You said You'd stay.
I Am that I Am, all things You are to me;
You became my Deliverer the day You set me free.
Counselor, Advocate, Wheel in the Middle of a Wheel,
You mean so much, to me You are so real!
Sweeter than honey, scripture says so;
Eternal life - my destiny, belief in You, is how I know.
Mighty God, Keeper, Shepherd, and Prince of Peace,
With You I am free, and my storms suddenly cease.
Everlasting Father, Calmer of the Sea,
In You I am complete, and all I hope to be!

So that we may boldly say, The Lord is my helper, and I will not fear what man shall do unto me.
Hebrews 13:6

You Are My Everything

Lost in sin, nowhere to turn;
In hell's fire, I was to burn.
Heard about a Man, who could pardon my debt;
So glad for salvation, I had nothing left.
Grace, so freely given to me;
Sufficient it was, to set me free.
My Deliverer, You are my Everything!
So many remembrances, I couldn't disregard;
Life's journey, was becoming unmistakably hard.
You'll put no more on us, than we can bear;
Life's trials are rough, but You are here.
To my own understanding, I must not lean;
For it is Your blood, that keeps me clean.
My Keeper, You are my Everything!
Sometimes the road, is filled with despair;
But to the Savior, I must draw near.
He comforts me, through the storm and rain;

He brings relief, that eases the pain.

Throughout the trials of life, He is a friend;

I'll forever rest in Him, until the end.

My Peace, You are my Everything!

Walking alone, with no one to share;

Asked the Lord, if He would care.

Promised to never forsake, or leave me;

Walk by faith, not by what I see.

He is The One that holds my hand;

My greatest companion, He understands.

My Friend, You are my Everything!

Out of all the possessions, that money can buy;

And every good thing, I can ever try,

He is the ultimate One, I won't ever deny;

And the only One, on whom I rely.

My Deliverer, My Keeper, My Peace, My Friend!

You Are My Everything!

But my God shall supply all your need according to His riches in glory by Christ Jesus.
Philippians 4:19

The Soon Coming King

Don't want to sit here idle, while time is passing by;
For if I remain in sin, my soul shall surely die!
For the soon coming King is closer than ever before;
He's given the ultimate sacrifice, so there is nothing more!
The Age of Grace is slowly ending, judgement will soon fall;
I must make a decision, either give nothing or my all!

Verily I say unto you, There be some standing here, which shall not taste of death, till they see the Son of Man coming in His kingdom. Matthew 16:28

Above All Else

There is no one else like You, I have searched high and low;
When the Lord needed a body, You said. "Send Me, I'll go!"
The angels nor man could offer the sacrifice You gave;
No greater love than to lay down Your life and make flesh behave.
Above all else I love You, though I just can't seem to get it right;
I keep trying to do it on my own, how can I follow without Your light.
I'm attempting to live holy on my own righteousness, which is filthy rags;
Through all of my accomplishments, I have the nerve to want to brag.
It's You that I must lean on, You are my Shelter through the storm and rain;
You are my Comforter, when I must endure heartache and pain.
Above all else I'll suffer, for this is what You have asked of me;
For that is the only true way, that I shall reign with thee!
There is no way my carnal mind can understand all the things You do;
In the spiritual realm, I can only worship God, when it is in truth!
Let this mind be in me which was also in Jesus Christ our Lord and King;
It is through Him, that we can have the victory in everything.
Above all else, you must love Him with your mind, soul, and heart;
Abide in Him and He'll abide in you, from you He will never depart!

He that cometh from above is above all: he that is of the earth is earthly, and speaketh of the earth:
He that cometh from Heaven is above all. John 3:31

To Really Know Me!

Do you really know me? I believe you think you do!
Just look at me and know, I am actually a part of you.
You will see that I'm not everything that I want to be;
You'll see I have problems too, trying to deal with me.
You'll know I came from a place, that many haven't seen;
The things I've been through, I cry, Lord make my heart clean.
If you knew me, you'd be amazed at what you actually see;
As a matter of fact, you'd be happy and laugh with glee.
You'd see we're not so different, and know we are the same;
Our problems we would share, and on each other place no blame.
We would know we are a peculiar people, set aside from the rest;
We would know we are the apple of God's eye and His very best!

For thou art an holy people unto the Lord thy God: the Lord thy God hath chosen thee to be a special people unto Himself, above all people that are upon the face of the earth. Deuteronomy 7:6

Holiness

*And that ye put on the new man, which after God is created
in righteousness and true holiness. Ephesians 4:24*

Holy Essence

Through the years, I'd gone astray;
The Lord saw fit, to spare me another day.
Caught up, and engulfed, in a world of sin;
I was lost, didn't know I could win.
Walked in a church, looking for hope;
So many years, at the end of my rope.
The Word of God came forth, with power and might;
I dropped to my knees, finally saw the light.
God came in, and manifested His presence;
He gave me understanding, of His "Holy Essence".
I will serve the Lord, throughout my days;
Surely, I'll acknowledge Him, in all my ways!

For they verily for a few days chastened us after their own pleasure; but He for our profit, that we might be partakers of His holiness. Hebrews 12:10

In the Likeness of You

Lord, I want to walk like you;
Tell me what I must do.
Lord, I want to see this thru;
How do I keep my walk true?
Lord, I want to have Your mind;
So, before all men, my light will shine!
Lord, I need to have Your ways;
So, I can follow You all my days!

So God created man in His own image, in the image of God created He him; male and female created He them. Genesis 1:27

Making You Like Me

I always wanted You, I knew it from the start;
Deep down inside, an emptiness filled my heart.
Evil was present, so I always chose the bad;
So many wrong decisions, which was all I had.
Not worthy of love, so I decided I didn't care;
But You never let it be, I still felt You there.
Felt like giving up, even declared I'd quit;
You helped me through, by pulling me out the miry pit.
All I did was say that's it, then You stepped right in;
Saved me from a devil's hell, snatched me out of sin.
Now that I'm with You, I can't straddle the fence;
Something keeps trying to tell me things, this makes no sense.
Deep down inside, a strong voice is crying out;
Just follow Me, please don't you ever doubt!
I'm not a man that I would lie, I told you that before;
All you did was knock and I opened up the door.
Just open your mouth, you can have what you ask;
No job too much for Me, I can handle any task.
Didn't I deliver you the day you began to seek?
Do you dare think that I'd leave you when you're weak?
In this my strength is made perfect, I'm making you like me;
Before your life ends, Christ-like is what you'll be!

Beloved, now are we the sons of God, and it doth not yet appear what we shall be: but we know that, when He shall appear, we shall be like Him; for we shall see Him as He is. 1 John 3:2

Leadership

*I am the Good Shepherd: the Good Shepherd
giveth His life for the sheep. John 10:11*

As We Follow Christ

Follow us as we follow Christ, they've said it from the start;
Loving them from the beginning, they have such genuine hearts.
Watching them go through their trials, praying they will stand;
Exemplifying the love of Christ, while extending a helping hand.
They sing their songs of Zion with so much power, you just shout;
You watch them give their all, living the life they preach about.
They epitomize the true love of Christ, no one can ever deny;
True faithful servants of God, on them we can fully rely.
These are they which plant and water, God lets the seeds grow high;
They say before you attempt anything else, please give my God a try.
Follow us as we follow Christ, it's just not the words they say;
It's the light that floods their eyes, when they preach and pray.
The way they love their neighbor, when rebuked and scorned;
The embrace they give all, when they are lonely and forlorn.
You witness how they persevere, through all their pain and strife;
Committed to living for Christ, they've dedicated their very life.
Though a host of enemies encamp about them, they never give in;
Urging us to live holy, and to shun the very appearance of sin.
Follow us as we follow Christ, holiness is the way we must live;
God gave His only begotten Son, our body is the least we can give.
They suffer persecution, which comes from the unlikeliest source;
Their souls remain anchored, as they stay on this narrow course.
On the raging waters, distress and peril on every side;
Nevertheless, they stand firmly, the Lord is their only guide.
Follow us as we follow Christ, this is our life of choice;
Found a friend in Jesus, and we will forever sing and rejoice.
Follow us as we follow Christ, this is what our leaders say;
Always giving God the glory, letting the Holy Spirit lead the way!

Be ye followers of me, even as I also [am] of Christ. 1 Corinthians 11:1

After God's Heart

After God's heart, seeking wholeheartedly to do His will;
Lying down in green pastures, led beside waters that are still.
Growing in character, as life's pressures become exceedingly great;
Never surrendering to the enemy, on the Lord, they patiently wait.
Hiding The Word in their heart, so against God they do not sin;
Meditating on it day and night, so they will be cleansed within.
It is a light unto their path, and a lamp unto their feet;
Oh, the taste of God's commandments, for they are so sweet.
Dwelling under the shadow of the Almighty, in the secret place;
Vessels of honor, humbling themselves to pray, seeking the Master's face.
Their steps are ordered by the Lord, God is their constant guide;
In the time of trouble, in His pavilion they safely hide.
After God's heart, they diligently care for His precious sheep;
They know He that keeps Israel does not slumber nor sleep.
Completed the Temple of God, when it remained undone;
God has promised you an eternal home, for your belief in His son.
Loving their neighbors and enemies as God told us to do;
For it is the very heart of the Master, that our leaders pursue.

Moreover thou shalt provide out of all the people able men, such as fear God, men of truth, hating covetousness; and place such over them, to be rulers of thousands, and rulers of hundreds, rulers of fifties, and rulers of tens. Exodus 18:21

Words Will Never Say

Mere words and expressions can never convey;
The things you've done, or what you portray.
Terms have limits, they only briefly describe;
The wonderful way, you are in my eyes.
Never have I met, two as one;
Who do all the things, you have done.
You carry yourselves, with beauty and grace;
Wisdom and holiness radiate in your face.
You always give credit, where it is due;
Knowing God has safely, brought you through.
Your life is the epitome of Jesus Christ's ways;
"Live holy is your motto, yes, everyday!"
You've taught me so much, in so little time;
By example you speak, and still in your prime.
I speak blessings on you, and your descendants as well;
Knowing God will richly bless you, and time will tell.
Keep living righteous, and always stay true;
I love you for all you do, and may God eternally bless you!

And the things that thou hast heard of me among many witnesses, the same commit thou to faithful men, who shall be able to teach others also. 2 Timothy 2:2

Well Done

Despise not the day of small beginnings, they declared this from the start;
Coming from such humble origins, a man and woman after God's own heart.
It won't always be this way, they said to each other in a tight embrace;
They knew the Savior would masterfully work it out, all fears He did erase.
Well done, my good and faithful servants, you are suffering the tribulations and trials;
Laid up for you is a crown of righteousness, it will all be over after a while.
Seek ye first the kingdom of God and His integrity, as the scripture says to do;
Never forsaking the Lord's promises, knowing that every one of them is true.
You shared your very last, as Jehovah Jireh, stretched your little into much;
Growing meekly in favor and grace, with the Almighty's gentle touch.
Never did you boast or brag, standing on the word and remaining steadfast;
Surviving the storm and the rain, knowing the test you would ultimately pass.
As others said you couldn't maintain, a small still voice says well done;
God looks deep within the inward parts, you are my daughters and sons.

Fighting for the souls of God's people, praying and fasting for all to make it in;
Loving every single sinner, and detesting and shunning the very appearance of sin.
Your pattern comes straight from the Bible, reproving and correcting the wrong;
Enduring through the hard times and struggles, as your Christian walk remains strong.
Well done is what that inner voice resonates, applauding a job executed so well;
Others speak so highly of your accomplishments, of your great acts they run and tell.
On the battlefield for the Lord, fighting until the task has been fully completed;
Never dissuaded to turn back, not once giving in to the fear of being defeated.
Remaining abased, the Lord exalts, the Spirit of Christ dwells deeply inside;
Holding on to His unchanging hand, never letting go, reverberating in your every stride.
Well done, good and faithful servant, how true and precious you will always be;
Loving you forever and always, the Creator says I'm so glad you decided to follow Me!

-------~\W\º©\º×Ö×Ö×º⁄∘○\W\-------

Neither as being lords over God's heritage, but being ensamples to the flock. 1 Peter 5:3

Take Care of Our Bishop

Deep within us he has sown so many spiritual things;
So, an abundance of carnal gifts, we readily and cheerfully bring.
Preach and live off the Gospel, the Bible proclaims he could do;
Yet never does he ask for himself, from me or from you.
Obedient to God, and he's highly ordained to preach the Word;
Help send him to the uttermost regions, so the Gospel can be heard.
Divine impartations, of which we can freely and heartily partake;
Heed the voice of the Lord, which causes Satan to tremble and shake.
Therefore, let us render to the Bishop, his just tribute and bequest;
For it is the will of God, and our humble and sincere request!

A bishop then must be blameless, the husband of one wife, vigilant, sober, of good behaviour, given to hospitality, apt to teach. 1 Timothy 3:2

Partners in The Gospel

Partners in the Gospel, as you run this Christian race;
Totally committed, as you endure with a steady pace.
Like Aquilla and Priscilla, living in this modern day;
Reaching out to others, upholding the Christian way.
Standing side by side, the Word hid deep in your hearts;
Sharing the teachings of Jesus, from it you won't part.
Giving thanks to you, as the Word convicts our slips;
As you preach with deep power, from your clay lips.
Our hearts so deeply pricked, we must confess and repent;
God uses His vessels, as the message is passionately sent.
Caring about souls is their business, is what you always say;
Laying hands, stirring up gifts, for the saints you constantly pray.
So, woman and man of God, double honor you are worth;
God called you to the ministry, even before your day of birth!

Two are better than one; because they have a good reward for their labour. Ecclesiastes 4:9

Love

Let all your things be done with charity. 1 Corinthians 16:14

Love the Lord

The Bible says: Love the Lord with all your heart;
Can't be taken away, because it's the good part.
This is what you declared you would do;
The Lord has really been good to you.
Don't you see the difference in your life;
It won't always be easy, there's stress and strife.
God honors faithfulness, He is forever true;
He can mend the broken heart, and make it new.
The word says: Love the Lord, completely;
His ever-present Spirit will fill you so sweetly.
God will never change, He is always the same;
Let your soul boast of His Wonderful and Holy name.
It is written: Love the Lord with all your mind;
His mercy endures forever, He is extraordinarily kind.
Live each and every day to make Heaven your goal;
And they tell me the half, has never ever been told!

Jesus said unto him, Thou shalt love the Lord thy God with all thy heart, and with all thy soul, and with all thy mind. Matthew 22:37

Love Is...

A life that was once lost;
A Savior that died, on a cross.
In Jesus, I have a friend;
My path to death did end.
God wiped my slate clean;
My sins are no longer seen.
Mercy that's new every day;
Grace helps me along the way.
Compassion, God has for me;
Your blood has set me free.
A Savior, that forgives my sins;
How He does it, again and again.
All that Jesus is, is my true love;
Descended down, from Heaven above.
On the throne, at the right side of God;
Making intercessions, to keep me free!

And from Jesus Christ, who is the faithful Witness, and the first begotten of the dead, and the Prince of the kings of the earth. Unto Him that loved us, and washed us from our sins in His own blood. Revelation 1:5

Love Made the Difference

Love made the difference for a sinner like me;
God in the flesh, who came to set us totally free.
He never sleeps or slumbers, He hears our every cry;
On Calvary He stretched His arms, on the cross He died.
Atonement for my offenses, when no other could be found;
None could pay the price, when we were completely bound.
A wonderful Savior, who lived to set a standard for creation;
Paid redemption's full price, to deliver people of every nation.
Love made the difference, when the payment was too high;
Sacrificial blood offerings of goats and bullocks couldn't satisfy.
He arose on the third day, this shows how much He truly cares;
Death was defeated, resurrection power profoundly shook the air.
Now I am the righteousness of God, He sees me as His own;
I can always call on Him, He promised to never leave me alone.
Love makes the difference, one day it changed me deep within;
It cleansed this impure heart and washed me wholesome from sin.
With loving kindness and mercy, it drew me to my Savior Divine;
I have a new outlook on life, it renewed and transformed my mind.
It is how you respond to your friends and your enemies too;
Even if you believe, they are doing the wrong thing to you.
It makes the difference, for it is directly from Heaven above;
It is the greatest weapon of our warfare, for God is absolute love.

Then said I, Lo, I come in the volume of the book it is written of Me, to do thy will, O God. Above when He said, Sacrifice and offering and burnt offerings and offering for sin thou wouldest not, neither hadst pleasure therein; which are offered by the law; Then said He, Lo, I come to do thy will, O God. He taketh away the first, that He may establish the second. Hebrews 10:7-9

The Love of Christ

The Love of Christ, is more than what you say;
It's the words that are uttered, when you pray.
The anointing you possess, that floods the place;
The very presence of God, radiates on your face.
It's the kind words you express, that turn away wrath;
Or the road you walk, that clears our path.
The presence of God, radiates on your face;
As the anointing you display, floods the place.
Interceding for us all, is your daily task;
Always willing to assist, if we only ask.
The Love of Christ is embodied, in all you do;
Staying meek and humble, as the Lord exalts you.
You may suffer persecution, on every side;
Yet you remain faithful, the Lord is your guide.
You've yielded to God's will, obedience is the key;
Consecrated every day, so your spirit remains free.
The Love of Christ, is what you so profoundly display;
May the Lord forever bless you, in a very special way!

And to know the love of Christ, which passeth knowledge, that ye might be filled with all the fullness of God. Ephesians 3:19

Who Will Love Me?

I've often wondered, but to my dismay;
Who will love me in a special way?
I've searched all my life, for so long;
So often I've chosen, what was wrong.
So many days, I wanted to go to God;
But the path seemed dark, and oh so hard.
So, I kept trusting in man, to satisfy my needs;
Trying to win his approval, with my good deeds.
My intentions were good, but my motives weren't right;
So, I smiled in the day, and cried all night.
A still small voice said, behold I am your Creator;
Besides Myself, there is no one that is greater.
I made you from dust and blew My breath in you;
Follow Me, and I will tell you just what to do.
For I love you eternally, and My love is true!

But God, who is rich in mercy, for His great love wherewith He loved us. Ephesians 2:4

Nothing Compares

To what or whom does Your love compare?
Of its depths, I shall never be aware.
I can't comprehend, why You died for me;
Or the price You paid to set me free.
Don't understand, why mercy has no price;
Or why Your grace, for my sins doth suffice.
Who can explain why on the cross You died;
Reconciling us back to God, You were crucified.
You came down from Heaven, to be our guide;
More than a man, the Lord with us, on You I rely.
Suffering so much pain, You never said a word;
Didn't pass Your cup, Your prayers were heard.
For so long, I'll strive so much to be like You;
A perfect example You are, Your likeness I'll pursue.
You loved the world, You are God's only begotten Son;
The battle You have fought, before it even begun.
How can I ever know why You died for me?
I'm filled with joy ever since You set me free!

For who in the Heaven can be compared unto the Lord? who among the sons of the mighty can be likened unto the Lord? Psalm 89:6

Marriage

*And they twain shall be one flesh: so then they are
no more twain, but one flesh. Mark 10:8*

I Complete You!

I complete you, do you believe that this is true?
I was taken from your rib, just to be with you.
You are my three in one, you've been really good to me;
You love me as Christ loves the church, with you I want to be.
I always dreamed of a man, that would someday win my heart;
We'd have a house full of children, it was beautiful from the start.
I was made to be your help meet, it's not good for man to be alone;
I'll love you for the rest of my life, today is our fifty-year milestone.
I saw you skipping down the street, your beauty drew me near;
I knew you would be my wife, to me you are so very dear.
Fifty years ago, I knew that you would be all that I need;
I felt that you would encourage and support as I took the lead.
It was more than your outer appearance that put my mind in a whirl;
You were my dream come true, you were my sweet little girl.
I always knew what I wanted, right from the very start;
After a half of a century, from you I still never want to part.
I'm so glad we made a vow to always be husband and wife;
Promising to love and cherish one another, for the rest of our lives.
We'll let no man put us asunder, our love is united by the Lord;
For it is virtually impossible, for anyone to break this threefold cord!

Therefore shall a man leave his father and his mother, and shall cleave unto his wife: and they shall be one flesh. Genesis 2:24

Spending My Life with You!

I've loved you since the tender age of nine, and it just won't go away;
I've tried to hide what I feel inside, but I believe it will always stay.
I love you dearly and I just can't lie, I often wonder if you think the same;
Even thought of being your wife, I wanted you to give me your name.
Been thinking of you lately, you even show up in my dreams at night;
We touch each other softly and gently, and it always seems so right.
No other man can do what you do for me, it doesn't appear to be real;
Just can't shake this attraction, it's so much more than what I feel.
I long to hold you and make this vow, to be the woman by your side;
Spending my life with you is what I want to do, what God has joined, no man can divide!

What therefore God hath joined together, let not man put asunder. Mark 10:9

I Missed You!

God woke me up this morning, sun brightly on my face;
As I searched my mind, worries left not a trace.
Thought about how I've been blessed, no chains to hinder me;
Thought about God's goodness, how He set me free.
Then I thought about your countenance, missed like I never knew;
Didn't know that I could feel the special way I do.
Some say that you get butterflies and a queasy feeling inside;
But my spirit's eased and mind renewed, my smile I just can't hide.
Love is more than a pitter-patter to know that it is true;
We're joined by God's love, that's what makes me for you!

Whoso findeth a wife findeth a good thing, and obtaineth favour of the LORD. Proverbs 18:22

Sharing My Heart with You!

⎯⎯⎯⎯⎯ ∽∾⊶⊷⊶⊷∾∽ ⎯⎯⎯⎯⎯

Since she was a youngster, there was something unique in her gaze;
Sometimes I'd sit and watch, utterly perplexed and amazed.
Such a special child, I knew she had a call from God above;
Bequeathed with gifts, not yet fully seen, the greatest one love.
Her unique strut is filled with elegance, sophistication, and style;
To look upon her countenance, always brings me a smile.
I love her with the love of God, for she's my very own;
I knew the day would come, when she'd become fully grown.
I know you know how much I love her, and I'm giving you her hand;
Here's a fragment of advice, so you'll please God, and be a loving man.
Love her as Christ loves the Church, be faithful, that's what you both deserve;
In her you have found a good thing, and the favor of the Lord you've earned.
Seek always to protect her, for she's so tender, gentle, and kind;
Above her, only love the Lord with all your heart, soul, and mind.
Continually trust in her, for she will remarkably enhance your life;
Stand beside her wholeheartedly, for you have found a virtuous wife.
Yes, I'm sharing my heart with you, for it's the right thing to do;
I believe that you will love my little girl, with a heart that's genuinely true!

⎯⎯⎯⎯⎯ ∽∾⊶⊷⊶⊷∾∽ ⎯⎯⎯⎯⎯

Husbands, love your wives, even as Christ also loved the church, and gave himself for it.
Ephesians 5:25

Our Pledge of Love

You are the woman that I've longed to be with, all of my life;
I've found such a good thing, ever since you became my wife.
Every moment that I look at you, I honestly thank God above;
It's you that I want to be with, it's you that I promise to love.
You hid yourself and lived holy, I'm glad you made the choice;
The Master did speak, and I was able to clearly hear His voice.
I'll love you as Christ loves the church, for the rest of my days;
Where He leads, I will follow and acknowledge Him in all my ways.
God wanted me to understand gentleness, so He sent me you;
You have done everything, and more that I needed a man to do.
An earthly love beyond my deepest belief, that I just could not foresee;
God knew you would be the one to come and take care of me.
I pledge to obey and cherish you, too, this is my solemn vow;
I'll be faithful and true, I shall declare this right here and now.
You are my husband, I sincerely adore you with all my heart;
For richer or poorer, for better or worse, until death do us part.
There is no love like God's, we've both found Him to be bona fide;
He said if we live in Him, then in us, He said He will abide.
We will never forget the day, He washed our sins as white as snow;
He made us whole, we are so glad, that He will never let us go.
Our blessed Savior, has purified this love that He has connected;
Teaching us that if we trust in Him, our love can only be perfected.
The Master has told us, that two flesh now have become as one;
We will always remember, the many wonders that He has done!

Nevertheless let every one of you in particular so love his wife even as himself; and the wife see that she reverence her husband. Ephesians 5:33

Obedience

If ye love me, keep my commandments. John 14:15

Obedience

If I am obedient, I shall eat the good of the land;
Why is this fact, so difficult for me to understand?
Obedience is better than sacrifice, You have said;
Yet, I continue to offer money and time instead.
No wonder I can't receive the things You have for me;
No wonder my vision is blurred, and I cannot see.
I walk as if You have not told me what I should do;
Yet I profess daily that my love for You is true.
How can I really say this and not obey Your voice?
Continuously yielding to flesh has been my choice.
Yet I cry out when everything around me falls apart;
Now, I genuinely ask You to transform my heart.
I want to sincerely follow You each and every way;
I want to be obedient to Your will, every single day.
I want to teach others, that Your way is right;
I want to win the battle in this spiritual fight.
I want to believe in my heart, all that You say;
I want to stay with You forever, and never stray.
I want to believe everything You declare that I am;
I want to know, how on the Word, I can firmly stand.
Lord, teach me to be obedient, so I can give my best;
Lord, teach me to be obedient, so I can pass every test!

Know ye not, that to whom ye yield yourselves servants to obey, his servants ye are to whom ye obey; whether of sin unto death, or of obedience unto righteousness? Romans 6:16

Teach Me

Teach me, so the Word I can hide in my heart;
Teach me, so when I grow older, from It I'll never depart.
Teach me, so that I will learn how to stand;
So even when I stray, on a firm foundation I'll land.
Let me know, I am a child of the King;
Then His praises, I will forever sing.
Let me know, I am the righteousness of God;
Then I will know, He can remove every scar.
Teach me, He is my very closest Friend;
Teach me to trust Him, so on Him I can depend.
Teach me to live holy, for He requires it of me;
Teach me, He's the One, who can truly set me free.
Let me know I am a conqueror, in Him, I can achieve;
Let me know in Him, I can do all things, if I only believe.
Let me know, I am the head, above and never beneath;
Let me know if I ask, in His will, my desires He'll bequeath.
Teach me how to love my brother, just like I love me;
Teach me He is my Father, and my soul He longs to free!

Teach me, O Lord, the way of thy statutes; and I shall keep it unto the end. Psalms 119:33

Praise And Worship

Make a joyful noise unto the LORD, all ye lands. Psalms 100:1

I Lift My Hands

I lift my hands in praise to You;
Because You gave Your all.
I lift my hands in praise to You;
Because You're on the throne.
I lift my hands in praise to You;
Because You are my Lord.
Jesus, the Son of God;
You know I adore You so.
I lift my voice in praise to You;
A sacrifice You gave.
I lift my voice in praise to You;
Because You made me whole.
I lift my voice in praise to You;
To sin, no longer a slave.
Jesus, the Son of God;
The Christ, My Lord and King,
I lift my hands in praise to you;
You are my all in all!

Hear the voice of my supplications, when I cry unto Thee, when I lift up my hands toward Thy holy oracle. Psalm 28:2

Only You

Only You can feed me daily bread, directly from on high;
Only You can give an answer, when the question is why?
My source of inspiration, help me love my neighbor as myself;
My source of consolation, You are my ever-present help.
Only You provide water, when my brook is running low;
Only You can give me shelter, when I'm surrounded by my foe.
My ultimate source of strength, whenever I am feeling weak;
My source of contentment, joy floods my soul when You speak.
Only You can fill the emptiness, that once inundated my soul;
You are my delightful Source, that now makes me whole!

Only the Lord had a delight in thy fathers to love them, and He chose their seed after them, even you above all people, as it is this day. Deuteronomy 10:15

This I Know!

············ᴡᴡ·⸰ᴄ⸝ꞯꞁᴏᴋꞯ⸝⸰·ᴡᴡ············

I'll never know why, God sent His only Son to die;
I'll not know, what makes the birds fly up in the sky.
No one really knows, why mercy is God's way;
Or why He chooses, to spare us another day.
No man knows the hour, when the Savior shall appear;
Nor, why so profoundly, for us He does care.
Many can attest to the fact, that He was crucified;
And profess to the fact, His people He's never denied.
So many confess, they never had a love so strong;
And we all know, that God can do no wrong.
Countless ways can't express, God's awesome ways;
But how many know, that He'll love us always!

ᴡᴡ·⸰ᴄ⸝ꞯꞁᴏᴋꞯ⸝⸰·ᴡᴡ

Know therefore this day, and consider it in thine heart, that the Lord He is God in Heaven above, and upon the earth beneath: there is none else. Deuteronomy 4:39

Prayer

Therefore, I say unto you, What things soever ye desire, when ye pray, believe that ye receive them, and ye shall have them. Mark 11:24

Prayer is the Key

Prayer is the key, I know because it works for me;
I take it to the altar and there He sets me free.
On my knees, I begin to pray;
Lord, You don't have to take it away.
Just give me the strength, so I can make it through;
Right now, I'm in need, of a touch from You.
You are my Strength and my Guide;
You said if I remain in You, then, in me You will abide!

Hear me when I call, O God of my righteousness: thou hast enlarged me when I was in distress; have mercy upon me, and hear my prayer. Psalm 4:1

Power of Prayer

Prayer can change anything, I've seen it done;
Out of the hands of the enemy, total victory is won.
It brings new essence to a life, that's been torn apart;
God will perform transformation, to any stony heart.
Yes, prayer changes everything, it happened to me;
Eyes were once wide shut, now they plainly see.
The road is not easy, and many times I have had to cry;
But I stand on the Word of God, for He dries my weeping eyes.
Prayer is the key, to a relationship with God;
Fall on your knees, for God, nothing is too hard.
You have to let the Holy Spirit, have His own way;
God will restore, all you have to do is pray!
Paul and Silas, locked in jail at midnight;
Prayed and praised, the Earth shook with a great might.
The prison doors opened, swinging really wide;
What must I do to be saved? The guard profusely cried.
Yes, prayer is the key, to the Divine Savior's love;
It's the only way to keep contact, with Heaven above!

Is any among you afflicted? let him pray. Is any merry? let him sing psalms. James 5:13

Just Pray

Pray without ceasing, is what we have been called to do;
Even for those who persecute, and despitefully use you.
We must ask God, for those things that we desire to be;
It shall be given, if we would just fall on our knees.
Humble ourselves, seek God's face, turn from wicked deeds;
Then, we'll hear from Heaven, God will supply our needs.
First, repent and we must really confess our sins;
God will cleanse and purify us, from the wrong within.
Boldly, going to the throne of grace, Father, Your perfect will be done;
Asking that our petitions, be granted, in the name of the Father's Son.
Morning, noon, and night, cry aloud, and He shall hear your voice;
Seek Him, with your whole heart, you'll find Him, make the choice.
Whatsoever ye ask in prayer, believe and you will receive;
With God, all things are possible, and in Him you can achieve!

Pray without ceasing. 1 Thessalonians 5:17

Good Morning Jesus

———————— ∿∾⊶⊰⊱⊷∾∿ ————————

Good Morning Jesus, thank you for another day;
I just wanted to speak, before I started on my way.
Please go before me, so that You can set the pace;
I want You to guide my footsteps, as I run this race.
Good Morning Jesus, I really just wanted to say Hi;
I'd like to do it early, so the day won't pass me by.
I think it's only right, to ask, how are You?
Before I begin the things that I want to do.
We'll talk during the day, but the morning time is special for me;
I'd like to acknowledge my Savior, on my bending knee!

———————— ∿∾⊶⊰⊱⊷∾∿ ————————

For, lo, as soon as the voice of thy salutation sounded in mine ears, the babe leaped in my womb for joy. Luke 1:44

Repentance

He that covereth his sins shall not prosper: but whoso confesseth and forsaketh them shall have mercy. Proverbs 28:13

Wash Me

I've asked for so much, that I cannot tell it all;
So often, have I stumbled, but You did not let me fall.
Every time, I opened my mouth, You heard my every call;
Now here I stand, and I'm bringing these burdens to You.
There is nothing else, that I really believe I can do;
So, here I am, You are the only One that can make me new.
To receive, just ask, seek, and knock, this is the key;
You came, not to condemn the world, but to set us free.
Now, I have but one request, Jesus, please, wash and purify me!

And I will cleanse them from all their iniquity, whereby they have sinned against Me; and I will pardon all their iniquities, whereby they have sinned, and whereby they have transgressed against Me. Jeremiah 33:8

Leaving the Past

Forgetting those things which are behind, like Paul said we must do;
Forgiving others and myself, for all that I've gone through.
Seeking the things of God, pressing for the prize in Jesus Christ;
Keeping my focus on the end, so that my gain is eternal life.
No looking at the cheering crowds, or those quickly running by;
Not leaning to my own understanding, on Christ I must rely.
Not concerned with being swift or strong, Lord, keep me in the race;
Even though I fall down, help me get up and maintain a steadfast pace.
Never thinking that I have apprehended, all the things needed to make it in;
Asking that I be armed with endurance, that is required for me to win.
Leaving the past behind, not dwelling on issues designed to hold me back;
I have to move forward, God has made me promises, He is by no means slack.
I'm reaching towards higher heights, that on my own I can never achieve;
With God as my Guide, every blessing, I shall humbly accept and receive!

Brethren, I count not myself to have apprehended: but this one thing I do, forgetting those things which are behind, and reaching forth unto those things which are before, I press toward the mark for the prize of the high calling of God in Christ Jesus. Philippians 3:13-14

Who Are You?

If you are saved than why do you,
Still do things the way you used to?
Who Are You?
I notice your walk has not changed;
The way you talk is mighty strange.
Who Are You?
Love your enemy is what you're told;
Not a word, do you utter, you're so cold.
Who Are You?
You open your mouth, to praise His name;
Same voice that gossips, things of shame.
Who Are You?
Shouting the victory, all over the church;
Through your window, neighbors watch you rehearse.
Who Are You?
Oh, so true, you used to be;
Now you're a hypocrite, wake up and see!
It's not who you are!

If a man say, I love God, and hateth his brother, he is a liar: for he that loveth not his brother whom he hath seen, how can he love God whom he hath not seen? 1 John 4:20

Salvation

Then said Jesus unto his disciples, If any man will come after Me, let him deny himself, and take up his cross, and follow Me. Matthew 16:24

An Open Invitation

An open invitation, this is what I give to you;
No need for hesitation, My love is pure and true.
I gave it to the Jews, but they declined, thinking I wasn't the one;
So, I offered it to the Gentiles, I am the only begotten Son.
I bid you to come to Me, from the highway near and far;
All you have to do is knock, the door is always ajar.
I'm waiting for you, with my arms stretched open wide;
Come running, safely in Me, you can forever abide.
An open invitation, it is freely given, so you can freely receive;
Those who come to the Father, in the Son they must believe.
I am the way, the truth, and the life, you must come through Me;
I am your redeemer, I can truly set you free.
I have no respect of person, why not heed the call?
It's not just for some, but, I'm presenting it to all.
The day you hear My voice, harden not your heart;
What can separate you from My love? What can keep us apart?

For ye are all the children of God by faith in Christ Jesus. Galatians 3:26

The Gift

God can mend a broken heart!
He puts together what's torn apart.
Life's got you down, nowhere to turn;
There's a gift from God, no one can earn.
Salvation is free for you and me;
Repent, Confess, Believe, that's the key!

Then Peter said unto them, Repent, and be baptized every one of you in the name of Jesus Christ for the remission of sins, and ye shall receive the gift of the Holy Ghost. Acts 2:38

Your Way of Escape

I am your Way of escape, you can come to Me;
I am your Everything, I can set you free.
Before you were formed in the womb, I knew what you'd do;
Still I came down from Heaven, just to rescue you.
I gave My life, so that sin would not have you bound;
I gave you the Word to live holy, so in it you could expound.
I created you in My likeness, I've always known just what you'd be;
I gave you the best example, so, holiness is what you'd plainly see.
I am your Way of escape, in Me is whom you should trust;
I put you high above all creation, when I formed you from the dust.
I am the Pathway to eternal life, I made you, I am your Elohim;
Walk by faith and not by sight, things are not always what they seem.
I'm your Way of escape, it's all working out for your good;
There is nothing too hard for Me, you've tried all that you could.
I will give you rest in that secret place, please abide in Me;
I came that you might have life so much more abundantly!

There hath no temptation taken you but such as is common to man: but God is faithful, Who will not suffer you to be tempted above that ye are able; but will with the temptation also make a way to escape, that ye may be able to bear it. 1 Corinthians 10:13

Precious to Me!

Your soul is so very precious to me;
Rubies and diamonds can never compete.
The whole world a man can seek to gain;
But losing his soul, will cause endless pain.
He can try to shuck, and slide by;
But the soul that sins, shall surely die.
Your soul is so very precious to me;
It's the part, that will live eternally.
Look to God, He can set you free;
Stay focused and be all you can be.
Your soul is so very precious to me;
Jesus died, so, this you would see!

To whom coming, as unto a living stone, disallowed indeed of men, but chosen of God, and precious. 1 Peter 2:4

A New Beginning

············᠁·◦-◠◡✕◯◯✕◠◡◦-·᠁············

A new beginning…
I must admit
I messed up a bit
I slid back
Totally off track
A war in my mind
Peace, I couldn't find
I looked to the hills
Turbulent waters stilled
A new beginning…
Now, I hate the act of sin
Since, I know I can win
With God on my side
Laying aside all pride
Prayer is the key
With Christ is where I'll be
Praise is on my tongue
It's only just begun
A new beginning…
It's a brand-new day!
For I know Jesus is the way
A new beginning!!!

············᠁·◦-◠◡✕◯◯✕◠◡◦-·᠁············

Though thy beginning was small, yet thy latter end should greatly increase. Job 8:7

Sanctification

But we are bound to give thanks alway to God for you, brethren beloved of the Lord, because God hath from the beginning chosen you to salvation through sanctification of the Spirit and belief of the truth. 2 Thessalonians 2:13

Think on These Things

⸺⸱৵৺০৻ᥫᥬ০৻৺৵⸱⸺

Think on these things, for it's the right thing to do;
Your mind functions better, on things that are true.
Thoughts are honest, and they will benefit you;
Your mind will continue to be thoroughly renewed.
Reflect on what is just, this will help you through;
Then, you can accomplish all that you pursue.
On everything that is pure, your spirit will stay clean;
To your own understanding, do not lean.
Love must continue to flood your heart and soul;
Healing all your hurts and wounds, making you whole.
A good report will uplift you, throughout the day;
Think on these things, so, God will direct your way!

⸺৵৺০৻ᥫᥬ০৻৺৵⸺

Be careful for nothing; but in everything by prayer and supplication with thanksgiving let your requests be made known unto God. And the peace of God, which passeth all understanding, shall keep your hearts and minds through Christ Jesus. Philippians 4:6-7

He Won't Let Me Go Out!

I guess you wonder, why I'm going out like this;
Tried doing it right, but my thoughts you'd dismiss.
Now, I'm coming full force and I just don't care;
You keep messing with me, now you'll feel the fear.
I tried to be humble, but, things are worse now;
You continue to push me, no longer do I bow.
I'm full of rage, I really don't want to behave;
Because I have an Adamic nature, and to sin I am a slave.
I feel like being buck wild, and living on the edge;
No longer will I comply, I'm really on the ledge.
I'm only hurting myself, that's what you say;
I regret everything I've done, but I won't sway.
You keep judging me, and shooting me down;
I want to live holy, but all you do is frown.
A small voice whispers, be still, for I am God;
Do you believe there is any task too hard?

I am not a man I should lie, nor need I repent;
I Am will do all, for that which I was sent.
I Am your Redeemer, I can set you free;
Jehovah Jireh, your Provider, I'm all you need.
I'm Elohim, I created you from the earth;
But to Me you are much more, than dust's worth.
I died to purchase you, from eternal demise;
A crown of life, will be, your everlasting prize.
I love you, don't you dare try to walk away;
I promise that I'd be with you, every single day.
How could you think I would forsake you?
Don't you know that My love is forever true?
I'm not like the rest, I'm closer than a friend;
Didn't I say rely on Me? On Me you can depend!
Don't you dare sit there feeling I walked out;
Give Me praise, let your voice let out a shout!

Blessed are the undefiled in the way, who walk in the law of the LORD. Psalms 119:1

My Longing

I've always believed in God, and dreamed of serving Him for so long;
But somehow, I became trapped, and the pleasures of sin were so strong.
I remember reading the Bible, and I knew that Jesus was the way;
But I strayed away, thinking tomorrow was just another day.
I went down the wrong road, and became burdened from the weight;
I kept calling on God's name, hoping that I wasn't too late.
For I knew I had no power to put it down, because in You, I did not abide;
Although I tried with all my might, to lay every weight aside.
Then I could handle no more, the indulgences were much too hard to bear;
I did not know what to do, it seemed as if no one cared.
I lifted my hands to Heaven, and cried Lord I'm in need of You;
I have nowhere else to go, and I just don't know what to do.
The Word of God is sure, it is a firm Foundation that's true;
I need to be saved and Holy Ghost filled, I know You can bring me through.
I slowly walked to the altar, I just knew He would bring me out;
I was standing on faith, in my heart I had no doubt.
He transformed my life that Sunday, so glad He did it for me;
Eyes that were once blind, now do plainly see!
As I travel this Christian way, can't say it has not been hard;
I've been bruised and battered, I've even suffered and been scarred.
I made a vow to trust and serve Him, for the rest of my years;
He has proven to be my Friend, and to me, He is so very dear!

One thing have I desired of the Lord, that will I seek after; that I may dwell in the house of the Lord all the days of my life, to behold the beauty of the Lord, and to enquire in His temple.
Psalm 27:4

Keep it Real!

Seems like the enemy, is forever, slowly creeping in;
You want to do right, but there is continually unrelenting sin.
This is the time, you should prevail firmly on God's word;
God's sheep know the Shepherd, His voice they've calmly heard.
Lo, I am with you always, you'll never walk alone;
You are going to make it, you are never on your own.
Problems overwhelm you, and burdens seem to get you down;
Look to the hills there's help, I AM, He said He'd turn it around.
You are an overcomer, He's the Lord, He'll safely see you through;
You can do all things through Christ, He will take care of you.
He's an ever-present Help, in the time of need;
With Him as your guide, you will always succeed.
The head and not the tail, above only and never beneath;
You are the righteousness of God, this He did bequeath.
On Christ the Solid Rock, you must stand, and by no means waver;
Don't bend or even yield, obtaining the Lord's earnest favor.
With all your heart you must trust in God, He will direct your way;
Lean not to your own understanding, with Him you must always stay.
Pressed down shaken together, it shall be given to you;
The windows of Heaven will open, the Lord's Word is forever true.
Walk by faith and not by sight, it's not about what you feel;
Stand on all the promises of God, that's the way you keep it real!

But the Lord said unto Samuel, Look not on his countenance, or on the height of his stature; because I have refused him: for the Lord seeth not as man seeth; for man looketh on the outward appearance, but the Lord looketh on the heart. 1 Samuel 16:7

Servitude

And He sat down, and called the twelve, and saith unto them, If any man desire to be first, the same shall be last of all, and servant of all. Mark 9:35

I Want to Serve Forever

I want to serve forever, it's the decision that I've made;
It took a while to reach it, but on my heart, it is now engraved.
No more halting between two opinions, I now know what is right;
I'm in this for the long haul, so I'm girding my loins for the fight.
Every act and every deed, must be done, because it is all unto the Lord;
No more expecting compensation, for Heaven is my just reward.
I want to serve forever, it is now embedded deep down in my soul;
I must follow Jesus, for He is the One who fulfilled the ultimate role.
I must love my enemy, though it has been extremely hard to do;
For the mind in me, is that of Christ, so it is wholehearted and true.
If I be faithful over a few things, I'll be ruler over so much more;
For there is no eye or ear, that has seen or heard, the things He has in store.
God came down from glory, to be wrapped in flesh, and dwell among man;
Showing us, we can overcome sin, and for righteousness we must stand.
I want to serve forever, Jesus humbly stated it best;
For the greatest among us are servants, this is the ultimate test!

And if it seems evil unto you to serve the LORD, choose you this day whom ye will serve; whether the gods which your fathers served that were on the other side of the flood, or the gods of the Amorites, in whose land ye dwell: but as for me and my house, we will serve the LORD. Joshua 24:15

Just to Be A Servant

Just to be a servant, is more than, you could ever ask;
For it carries great responsibility, it is a major task.
Forsaking all earthly riches, to follow the Good Master;
Giving your treasures, that's stored in your box of alabaster.
Not just a hearer of the Word, but you are also a doer too;
You live by the Word of God, for you know the Bible is true.
You are a cheerful giver, and so loving and so kind;
You think on the things of Christ, as a result, He keeps your mind.
You are a minister of the Gospel, preaching what you live;
Sharing with others, of yourself you always freely give.
Just to be a servant, you have humbly answered the call;
God will continue to exalt you, as you learn to surrender all!

If any man serve Me, let him follow Me; and where I am, there shall also My servant be: if any man serve Me, him will My Father honour. John 12:26

Just A Token

I just want to express my gratitude, for each and everything you do;
Your thoughtful gestures of kindness, say so much about you.
The time you take to prepare and plan, reveals your loving touch;
With every thought and deed, shows the depth of just how much.
You always have a smile and kind word, despite your many tasks;
You continuously give of yourself, most of the time, I don't even ask.
So, let these words serve as a reminder, for they are only a token;
For I am only trying to express my thoughts, which are seldom spoken!

Submitting yourselves one to another in the fear of God. Ephesians 5:21

A Christian Warrior

A Christian warrior, armed for battle, with the Word that's sharper than any two-edged sword;
A living and powerful weapon, cutting bone from marrow, straight from the Lord.
Wrestling not against flesh, but against principalities, and rulers of darkness in high places;
Against spiritual hosts of wickedness, lurking in this dominion, even in the most remote spaces.
Like Jesus on the mount, using Scripture to reject temptations from Satan, who rules the very air;
Simply saying "It is written," for by no other words, does he show the slightest fear.
Anger and the wrath of man, will not suffice, for it doesn't show the righteousness of God above;
So, a true Christian warrior, must fight God's way, and that is simply by showing love.

Thou therefore endure hardness, as a good soldier of Jesus Christ. 2 Timothy 2:3

Stay in The Church

Stay in the church, it is where you will find your aid;
It's a hospital for the sick, the bill is already paid.
It's where you get strength, so that you can go through;
It provides the answers, to any problems, that are ailing you.
Stay in the church, saints gather from far and near;
Remember, Christ holds the church, so very dear.
Upon this rock I'll build it, the gates of Hell won't prevail;
You'll be endowed with power, the head and not the tail.
Stay in the church, the word is always being taught;
When in yokes and bondages, you will not be caught.
Stand in the liberty, wherewith Christ hath made you free;
Enter into His gates, with praise, is all God is asking of thee.
Stay in the church, there is nowhere to run if you leave;
Stay and all of God's promises, you will surely receive.

Not forsaking the assembling of ourselves together, as the manner of some is; but exhorting one another: and so much the more, as ye see the day approaching. Hebrews 10:25

Thankfulness

In everything give thanks: for this is the will of
God in Christ Jesus concerning you.
1 Thessalonians 5:18

Thank You

So much has happened, I cannot tell it all;
God picked me up, after every fall.
He consoled me, when the hurt was deep;
Lovingly soothed the pain, He even let me weep.
Not like the nine, who showed no gratitude;
Gratefulness is from You, please change my attitude!
I may have said it, for all the things, You've done before;
But this time it's for everything, that You have in store.
Genuine and heartfelt, this is coming from deep within;
I bless Your Holy Name, for protecting me from sin.
I appreciate everything, You've been real, real, good;
Even though, I didn't do, everything I should.
Heartfelt thanks, is what I would like to express to You;
You've remained faithful, still doing what You need to do.
So, I thank You, for always carrying me through;
I appreciate Your mercies, for everyday they are new!

And one of them, when he saw that he was healed, turned back, and with a loud voice glorified God,
And fell down on his face at His feet, giving Him thanks: and he was Samaritan. Luke 17:15-16

Thoughts of Thanks

In all things, give thanks, this is what He would have you to do;
Praising God continually, for all that you will ever go through.
He is good, and His mercy endures forever and always;
O bless, His holy and righteous Name, for all of your days.
For we must praise and worship Him, with our whole heart;
In everything giving thanks, for we must do our part!

Let us come before His presence with thanksgiving; Let us shout joyfully to Him with psalms.
For the Lord is the great God, And the great King above all gods. Psalm 95:2-3

Trust

Delight thyself also in the LORD; and He shall give thee the desires of thine heart.
Psalms 37:4

Believe

You said so many things, and I believe that they are true;
When all else fails, You said I could count on You.
But here I stand, with my back to the wall;
You said You would be there when I fall.
A broken heart, it doesn't seem to mend;
Strong like an oak tree, so I don't even bend.
So tired of hurting, so I'll just go my own way;
How will it be different, from any other day?
So, I'll just stay here, in the cold and rain;
And walk away, because I can no longer remain.
A voice deep inside, cries out, do you believe I am God?
Do you remember what I said? For me, nothing is too hard.
I resist the proud, but the humble I embrace;
Stop believing in yourself, and let Me set the pace.
Rely on Me totally, I'll be the one to help you thru;
There is none to be found, that loves you like I do.
Surrender all, I am God, I know how you feel;
I'll be here during it all, because I love you for real!

And all things, whatsoever ye shall ask in prayer, believing, ye shall receive. Matthew 21:22

Holding On!

Trying to hold on, You said when I'm weak, You are strong!
Suddenly the burden seems heavy, the road is so very long.
I don't mind waiting, I've sang that song from my heart;
Yet, I'm growing impatient, but from You, I can't depart.
You gave me free will, I am allowed to do what I decide;
Yet, the voices from the past, are growing stronger inside.
I'm standing all alone, and I never thought I'd be here;
You are the strength of my life, of whom shall I fear?
Said You'd never leave me or forsake me, a guide You'd be;
I've got to depend on my faith, for this situation, is not what I see.
Mother always prays, that we're not moved by circumstance;
God, I'm trusting You, with no other, will I take a chance.
Yes, I can hold out, for there is no other help I know;
For with all my heart, soul and mind, I put my trust in You!

But I trusted in Thee, O LORD: I said, Thou art my God. Psalms 31:14

Trust in God

So, You tell me I should trust You;
That's just what I want to do.
Even though the pain is great;
I promised that I would wait.
Carnality is blinding me;
It's hard to see the victory.
Still, I'll bless You the more;
For this is what I was created for.
But, doubt is slowly creeping in;
You fight the battle, then I'll win.
Circumstances are looking bleak;
God of Heaven, it's Your face I seek.
I need answers, that only You know;
Went to my earthly aid, now to You I go.
Trust in God, He's a faithful friend;
My spirit will serve Him until the end.
Though He slay me, yet will I trust God;
Thru the trying times, even when it's hard.
Not my understanding, You direct my ways;
I will trust You, for the rest of my days!

And he believed in the Lord; and He counted it to him for righteousness. Genesis 15:6

Lord, Help My Unbelief!

Lord, I've cried out, I believe, but, please help my unbelief;
I keep choosing not to obey, and it's only causing me grief.
I've chosen the low road, because it's all that I know;
You're calling me to the inner courts, but to the outer courts I go.
I've seen Your wonder working power, of it I have no doubt;
Time after time, I've witnessed, how You've brought me out.
Deep in my heart, I've constantly struggled with my stubborn ways;
I'm giving them up, for You deserve all the glory, honor, and praise.
If I would just surrender my will, and give it over to You;
I must learn to trust in the fact, that You are faithful and true!
Love my neighbor as myself, seems like such a simple task;
Yet I remain persistent, and refuse to do just what You ask!
Evil for evil, vengeance is mine, declares the Lord of Hosts;
But if you mess with me, I'll get you back, of this I relentlessly boast.
I never thought I'd be in this place, so, my heart is deeply grieved;
Lord all I can ask, is take me back, to where I first believed.
I need a touch from You, like I've never needed before;
I know I've said this previously, but I need it now even more.
Help my unbelief, for I need to please You, Father above;
It is my earnest desire to please You, and show You my undying love!

And straightway the father of the child cried out, and said with tears, Lord, I believe; help thou mine unbelief. Mark 9:24

Victory

*But thanks be to God, which giveth us the victory
through our Lord Jesus Christ.*
1 Corinthians 15:57

Victory Over the Enemy

Victory over the enemy, that's what I seek to attain;
My eyes are on the prize, looking to obtain eternal gain.
As spiritual wickedness in high places, try to overtake me;
For fighting against flesh and blood, no, that's not the key.
Casting down every imagination, that exalts itself against God;
Yet, letting my mind, think heavenly things, seems to be so hard.
Yet, I remain wise as a serpent, yet harmless as a dove;
For the Holy Spirit is with me, guiding me in truth and love.
More than a conqueror, as I put my trust in the Master above!

But thanks be to God, which giveth us the victory through our Lord Jesus Christ.
I Corinthians 15:57

I Am an Overcomer

I am an overcomer; I will be of good cheer;
I'm enduring the tribulations, but of this I am aware.
Jesus suffered; and with Him I want to reign;
I, too, will undergo heartaches, and there will be pain.
I am an overcomer, just take a look and see;
He said, if I abide in Him, then He will abide in me.
Greater is He that is in me, than he that is in the earth;
Above every other creature, He values my worth.
Forgetting those things, and leaving the past behind;
He has restored my soul, and renewed my mind.
He promised, that He will never leave me alone;
He is my Alpha and Omega, He is my Chief Cornerstone.
I am an overcomer, He calls me His very own;
I'll safely rest in Him, He pitied my every groan.
He told me, I'm the head and not the tail;
In Him, I can do all things, He won't let me fail.
He said that I'm above, and never below;
I can't be plucked from His hand, He won't let me go.
I am an overcomer, Satan no longer holds the deed;
Whom the Son sets free is free indeed, God supplies every need!

Fight the good fight of faith, lay hold on eternal life, whereunto thou art also called, and hast professed a good profession before many witnesses. 1 Timothy 6:12

Overcoming People

·········∿·◦◦᠐◦◯◯◦᠐◦◦·∿··········

Overcoming people, is really not that difficult for someone to do;
The genuine test comes, when removing things hindering my walk with You.
But it's my own evil and lusts, that are separating us now;
I'm throwing my hands in the air crying "Lord, I can't imagine how."
People you want to surmount, is like a mirror in which you can see;
What God begins to show you, is that which will truly set you free.
The things you view in others, that sometimes upset you deep within;
These are some of the conflicting issues, that can arise causing you to sin.
Don't focus on overcoming people, work on the dilemmas that obstruct your stand;
Keep your eyes looking to Jesus, and reaching the Promised Land!

·········∿·◦◦᠐◦◯◯◦᠐◦◦·∿··········

Ye are of God, little children, and have overcome them: because greater is He that is in you, than he that is in the world. 1 John 4:4

Good Judgement Call

I want to make decisions, strictly based on what God says is true and right;
When I'm confused and bewildered, I want to do what is pleasing in His sight.
Please don't let me be like Jonathan, when he chose Saul over David to follow;
Destruction was his end, that would be a pill too hard for me to swallow.
Lord, I know I've made mistakes, and they are too plentiful to even try to say;
But, I'm begging and pleading to You, because only You can make a way.
Based on my emotions and feelings, I'll always choose the wrong thing to do;
But with Your Word, hid deep inside my heart, it is my desire to please You.
Give me good judgement, so I can choose to do just what You want me to;
Then I will be fully committed, and to You I will remain forever true!

Teach me good judgment and knowledge: for I have believed thy commandments. Psalm 119:66

Passing the Test

Life brings tribulations, that we feel we cannot bear;
We must rely on God, so, we will not be overtaken by fear.
Be of good cheer, Jesus overcame the world, so can we;
He came that we might have life more abundantly.
Tests come to increase our faith, and to make us strong;
Wait patiently on God, He will come, and it won't be long.
Pass the test, for in Him are deeper depths and higher heights;
Joy comes in the morning, although tears may cloud your nights.
Just go through, God will do everything, He promised He would;
You will be victorious, for on the Word of the Lord, you've stood!

And He said, Take now thy son, thine only son Isaac, whom thou lovest, and get thee into the land of Moriah; and offer him there for a burnt offering upon one of the mountains which I will tell thee of. Genesis 22:2

Joy Comes in the Morning

I have had my share of troubles, the trials have not been few;
While under the influence of Jesus, there were things I had to do.
The road has been long, and I've hit a pothole or two;
God has been mighty good, and His love has been faithful and true.
Can't say, I have the testimony that I was saved in my younger years;
But, nothing is too hard for God, for He continues to dry my tears.
Yes, I can say I've lived a good life; and these words I can humbly say;
I'll make it in those Pearly Gates, for in the Word I'll stay.
So, my midnight has ended, and joy has come for me;
Because, forever in His loving arms, is where I want to be!

For His anger endureth but a moment; in His favour is life: weeping may endure for a night, but joy cometh in the morning. Psalm 30:5

Running this Race

I'd tell you I'd bench press the max, if you'd ask me if I'm strong;
I believe I could run distances, that many would admit were very long.
I might even be able to outrun, the fastest supersonic jet;
I think I could throw a disc so far, new records would be set.
But this battle I'm in, is not given, to the swift nor the tough;
In reality, the faster I go, might make the road most rough.
This event requires endurance, so I must keep a steady pace;
I'll look to the hills for my help, so that I may stay in this race.
He told me to trust in Him, His Word in my heart I must hide;
I must be in constant training, for only God can lead and guide.
I will keep my body under subjection, a castaway I cannot be;
After preaching to others, I must remember to take care of me.
I am running with such assurance, with my focus on the prize;
I'm not staring at diversions, on the trophy, I have fixed my eyes.
An incorruptible crown of eternal life, I am seeking to obtain;
For it is truly my soul's desire, that with Him, I shall reign!

Wherefore seeing we also are compassed about with so great a cloud of witnesses, let us lay aside every weight, and the sin which doth so easily beset us, and let us run with patience the race that is set before us, Hebrews 12:1

No More Running

-------˓ⅿⅿˑ-ⓞ-ⓝⓔⓨⓞ♦ⓞⓨⓔ-ⓞ-ⓞ-ⅿ--------

The Bible says, Resist the devil, and it is he who will have to flee;
I'm scratching my head wondering, why is he always running me?
Is it because I'm not trying to resist, but I'm really just giving in;
Not realizing, the power of the Holy Spirit that lies deep within?
Stand still and let the Lord fight the battle, is what I must do,
I keep insisting I can handle the situation, so the test is renewed.
I have to run this race with patience, but that's something I need;
This time, when you speak to give me guidance, I will take heed.
I'll stop scampering around, full of so many fears and doubts;
I'll look to the Lord, for He is the One who can provide the way out.
He is my Comforter, Provider, Deliverer and my very Best Friend;
No more running, God is the One, who will be with me, until the end!

-------ⅿⅿ-ⓞ-ⓝⓔⓨⓞ♦ⓞⓨⓔ-ⓞ-ⓞ-ⅿ-------

Know ye not that they which run in a race run all, but one receiveth the prize? So run, that ye may obtain. 1 Corinthians 9:24

The War Is On!

We're in a state of war, this is the devil's final hour;
He's going to and from, seeking whom he may devour.
He preys upon the weak, he tries to deceive the very elect;
If you don't have your shield and armor, it's you he will select.
The heat has been turned up high, the pressure is real;
No time for tears, Satan seeks to destroy, kill, and steal.
He knows his time is up, he has summoned demonic forces;
You must be spiritual, relying on all heavenly sources.
He's even in the church, he's so cunning in his hiding place;
Everyone is blaming each other, they fail to see his face.
His strategy is well planned, he has some leaving the scene;
They have decided that living holy, is beyond their means.
He is posing as an angel of light, he's very hard to see;
You can easily be seduced, and this just shouldn't be.
He is causing division amongst brethren, when he is around;
Gird up your loins, so you can firmly stand on solid ground.
Pray for the saints, so they will not fall by the wayside;
Be not dismayed, he was defeated when Christ was crucified.
Open your spiritual eyes, so his cover will be fully blown;
Trust in the Word and His promises, the seed has been sown.
Hold on to Jesus, no one can pluck you from His hand;
He is a solid rock, on Him you must always stand!

Yea, and all that will live godly in Christ Jesus shall suffer persecution. 2 Timothy 3:12

Eyes Have Not Seen

Eyes have not seen, all that God has prepared for me;
Ears have not heard, the things that will come to be.
His ways are so high, above the manner in which I behave;
His thoughts are so different, instead of those in which I engage.
There is none like Him, in the Heavens above, nor the Earth below;
When I am discouraged and despondent, it is to Him that I can go.
He has promised, that He will be my constant friend;
He has assured me, that it is upon Him, I can depend.
I never imagined, that I would find a Father so dear;
Even when I am unfaithful, He has been right there.
My heart has never felt a love, that is so pure and true;
His touch is so soothing, and He knows just what to do.
I'm covered by His precious blood, in Him my protection lies;
In Him I've placed my trust, for He is sovereign and wise.
Eyes have not seen, what I shall earn, if I remain with Thee;
Ears have not heard, what You have in store, just for me!

"But as it is written, Eye hath not seen, nor ear heard, neither have entered into the heart of man, the things which God hath prepared for them that love Him." 1 Corinthians 2:9

Encouraging the Saints

Encourage the saints, who pave the way;
Interceding for all, as they kneel and pray.
Satan attacks, and tries hard to intervene;
Righteous prayers avail, demons flee the scene.
We are all one body, our head is Jesus Christ;
He is our Savior, He paid the ultimate price.
So, as we love ourselves, let us love one another;
When you hurt, I hurt, for we are sisters and brothers.
Encourage the saints, who are newborn babes in Christ;
We must be strong, so they can endure and survive.
Teach them how to avoid, the devices of the evil one;
Then, they can run this race and hear the words, well done.
They have to know that God loves them, unconditionally;
All they have to do is believe, that the Son is the key.
Lift them up, when they are feeling down and out;
Let them know what being a Christian is all about.
Encourage the saints, who God has placed in command;
Upholding their vision, behind them we firmly stand.
Accepting rebuke, as they reprove and correct;
This is their job, so that the saints stay in check.
We must always honor them, because honor is due;
Then, they can preach the gospel, as souls they pursue.
Take care of them, and the Lord will take care of you;
Above your reasonable service, more is required to do.
Encourage one another, that's how we'll all make it in;
If you see me falling short, don't you dare laugh or grin.
Please take the time to support me, as I go through;
One can chase a thousand, but ten thousand flee from two!

These things I have spoken unto you, that in Me ye might have peace. In the world ye shall have tribulation: but be of good cheer; I have overcome the world. John 16:33

Wisdom

If any of you lack wisdom, let him ask of God, that giveth to all men liberally, and upbraideth not; and it shall be given him. James 1:5

Fear God

Down through the years, I think, I've dreaded so much stuff;
The tests that have happened, have been exceptionally tough.
I've worried about man, who had no place for my soul;
I really, did not consider the fact that God is in control.
How could I not fear, the one who can cast me into Hell?
I never wanted that to be, the eternal resting place, I'd dwell.
Yet, I seldom shunned evil, I yielded to its enticing advances;
Every opportunity I'd get, I was willing to take my share of chances.
Now, a fool is what I am, and I stand in a desolate location;
God is the only source, which can alleviate this crucial situation.
Now, I'll learn to follow His ways, even if I don't understand;
For He means more to me, than my self-concocted plans.
I'll seek wisdom through the Scriptures, for divine insight;
So that I can endure and remain, in this spiritual fight.
I'll be a hearer and a doer of the Word, the rest of my years;
The fear of God will help me listen, with my spiritual ears.

Let us hear the conclusion of the whole matter: Fear God, and keep His commandments: for this [is] the whole [duty] of man. Ecclesiastes 12:13

A Woman of Wisdom

Standing on a firm foundation, prayer gives you direction of what to do;
In constant communication with the Savior, your relationship is true.
He speaks to you daily, letting you know that He is a friend;
You are a humble servant, devout and dedicated until the end.
Growing in prudence daily, feeding us food that comes from on high;
Not just a hearer but a doer, to your life the Word you directly apply.
Wisdom flows from your mouth like a stream, clarity it seems to bring;
The revelation knowledge that you possess, can only come from the King.
As I sit in sheer wonder, I realize that I too would love to have this guarantee;
For women of wisdom operate in power, they are not in awe over what they see.
Not complaining or mumbling a single word, their Christian character they uphold;
Going through the fiery trials of life, God brings them through as pure gold.
Not moved by circumstances, but by faith in the Master, obedience is the key;
A woman of wisdom is what I notice in you, and every day is what I shall strive to be!

Who can find a virtuous woman? For her price is far above rubies. Proverbs 31:10

A Virtuous Woman

Rising early in the morning, preparing for the day;
Good morning Jesus, kneeling down to pray.
Intimate relationship, when she speaks to God above;
Declaring victory over the enemy, fiercest weapon – love.
Affectionately greets her husband, start of a brand-new day;
Children proclaim, "She's blessed", embraces launch her way.
Wisdom guides her footsteps, for the many tasks she'll do;
Watching and praying, her Savior safely guides her through.
Worth more than the cost of rubies or diamonds could ever be;
Her light shines before men, so that the entire world can see.
Never boastful or proud of her deeds, knowing it's God's Grace;
Feet prepared with the gospel of peace, to run this Christian race.
An angel in our midst, always helping others to make it through;
Who can find a virtuous woman? We've found one in you!

Her children arise up, and call her blessed; her husband also, and he praiseth her. Proverbs 31:28

For You

A woman of wisdom, for this is given to those who ask;
Overtaken by her fervor, for she refuses to wear the mask.
Sometimes mistaken, for she has often had to stand alone;
So, others misconstrue her heart, to be one of stone.
Your eyes tell a different story, sometimes I can see the pain;
Delay is not denial, my dear sister, your struggle is not in vain.
God wants you to yield your will, your spirit He's not trying to break;
He's refining you on the potter's wheel, a vessel of honor He wants to make!

Every wise woman buildeth her house: but the foolish plucketh it down with her hands.
Proverbs 14:1

Printed in the United States
By Bookmasters